Bonsai Book for Beginners

Learn How to Plant, Grow, and Care for a Bonsai Tree Step by Step

© Copyright Robert Smith - All rights reserved.

The content contained within this book may not be reproduced, duplicated or transmitted without direct written permission from the author or the publisher.

Under no circumstances will any blame or legal responsibility be held against the publisher, or author, for any damages, reparation, or monetary loss due to the information contained within this book, either directly or indirectly.

Legal Notice:

This book is copyright protected. It is only for personal use. You cannot amend, distribute, sell, use, quote or paraphrase any part, or the content within this book, without the consent of the author or publisher.

Disclaimer Notice:

Please note the information contained within this document is for educational and entertainment purposes only. All effort has been executed to present accurate, up to date, reliable, complete information. No warranties of any kind are declared or implied. Readers acknowledge that the author is not engaged in the rendering of legal, financial, medical or professional advice. The content within this book has been derived from various sources. Please consult a licensed professional before attempting any techniques outlined in this book.

By reading this document, the reader agrees that under no circumstances is the author responsible for any losses, direct or indirect, that are incurred as a result of the use of the information contained within this document, including, but not limited to, errors, omissions, or inaccuracies.

Table of Contents

INTRODUCTION	1
CHAPTER 1: THE HISTORY AND TRADITION OF BONSAI	4
A MINIATURE HISTORY LESSON	4
THE PHILOSOPHY BEHIND BONSAI	8
TRADITIONS	10
CHAPTER 2: TYPES OF BONSAI TREES	11
POPULAR BONSAI GROWING STYLES	11
Moyogi, or "The Curve Style"	11
Ishizuki, or "The Rock Growing Style"	11
Bunjingi, or "The Literati Style"	12
Hokidachi, or "The Upright Broom Style"	13
Fukinagashi, or "The Windswept Style" or "The Windblown Style"	13
Kengai, or "The Cascading Style" or "The Bent Tree Style"	14
Han-kengai, or "The Semi-Cascading Style"	14
Bankan, or "The Coiled Style"	15
Shakan, or "The Slanting Style"	15
Chokkan, or "The Typical Upright Style"	15
Netsuranari, or "The Spreading Shape"	16
Ikadabuki, or "The Raft Style"	16
Kadushi, or "The Open Raft Style"	16
Sankan, or "The Fork Style"	17
Sokan, or "The Split Style"	17
Kabudachi, or "The Multi-Trunk Style"	18
Yose-ue, or "The Forest Style"	18
Seki-joju, or "The Growing on a Rock Style"	18
BONSAI TRADITION	18
ANATOMY OF A BONSAI	19
Pot or Container	19
Foliage	20
Branches	20
Trunk	20
Roots	21

CHAPTER 3: SELECTING YOUR BONSAI — 22

How Can You Find Your Future Bonsai? — 22
- The Indoor or Outdoor Dilemma — 24
- Size Matters — 25
- Selecting the Pot — 26

Using Seeds to Grow — 28
- Wild Seeds — 28
- Commercial Seeds — 29
- Planting Seeds — 29
- Stratification of Seeds — 30
- Sowing The Seed — 30

Understanding Containers — 31

Plant Propagation — 33
- Layering — 33
- Cutting — 34

CHAPTER 4: CARE GUIDE FOR YOUR BONSAI — 35

Feeding — 35
Placement — 39
Spraying — 42
Repotting — 42
- How to Remove the Bonsai from the Pot? — 44
- Soil Checkup — 44
- Cleaning Roots — 44
- Pruning the Roots — 45
- The Repotting Process — 46
- Repotting Entire Bonsai Trees — 47
- Initial Care For Repotted Bonsai — 48

Watering — 49
Long-Term Bonsai Care — 51
- Soil — 52
- Pot — 52

Bonsai Damage — 53
- Leaf Bud Damage — 53
- Leaf Damage — 54
- Branch Damage — 55

Soil Conditions — 56
- Basic Checks — 56
- Loose Soil — 56
- White Growth — 57

CHAPTER 5: STYLING AND SHAPING YOUR BONSAI — 58

- PRUNING — 58
  - *Branch or Twig Pruning* — *60*
  - *Debudding* — *60*
  - *Leaf Trimming* — *60*
  - *Shoot Pinching or Cutting* — *60*
- WIRING — 61
- AGEING — 63
- TRIMMING — 64
- MANURING — 64
- CHOOSING THE POT — 65

CHAPTER 6: PEST, INFECTION, AND DISEASE REMEDIES — 68

- INSECTICIDES — 70
- PESTS — 71
  - *Ants* — *71*
  - *Aphids* — *73*
  - *Caterpillars* — *75*
  - *Boring Insects* — *76*
  - *Earthworms* — *79*
  - *Larvae of May Beetles* — *80*
  - *Mealy Bugs* — *81*
  - *Red Spiders* — *82*
  - *Scale Insects* — *83*
- DISEASES — 83
  - *Powdery Mildew* — *83*
  - *Rust* — *85*
  - *Diseases Caused by Nutrient Deficiency* — *86*
  - *Root Rot* — *87*

CHAPTER 7: STYLE GUIDE — 89

- CHOOSING THE RIGHT STYLE OF BONSAI — 89
  - *What to Look for when Choosing a Bonsai Tree* — *91*
- HOW SHOULD YOU DISPLAY IT? — 93
- PRESENTATION TIP — 95
  - *The Formal Style* — *95*
  - *The Semi-Formal Style* — *96*
  - *Informal Style* — *97*
- HARVESTING FOR YOUR KITCHEN — 98

CONCLUSION — 99

Introduction

You are going to have a tree in your house.

That is unless you already have a bonsai, in which case, you already have a tree in your house. And yes, a bonsai is a tree, much like what you see in the forests, your backyard, or in the woods. Some people like to call them plants due to their small stature, and that's okay too. Whatever you think they are, what really matters is what the bonsai helps to create in your room or wherever they are placed: a sense of beauty and awe.

If you ask me why I consider them trees, it has everything to do with the general anatomy of a tree. At the most foundational level, a tree consists of a crown, a trunk, and roots. A bonsai has a similar foundation. It is still quite difficult to pinpoint exactly what makes a bonsai a bonsai, which is why many people think of them as miniature trees. As I mentioned earlier, it is okay to think of them as plants as well.

However, they are not grown in the same way that you would a typical plant or an herb. It isn't simply about planting seeds, watering them, and giving them the occasional sunlight. There is more to growing a bonsai tree, which you can understand when you look at the result: a beautiful addition to your home that is quite frankly something no other plant or ornament can provide. Plus, they live for a very long time.

Oh yes, a bonsai tree has a long life. A common misconception is that since bonsai trees are so small, their physical stature reflects their lifespan. Reality presents a scenario that is quite the contrary. Did you know that the Ficus tree carefully maintained in the Crespi Bonsai Museum is over 1,000 years old? Pretty amazing, isn't it? Bonsai trees may actually outlive us and our children, and their children as well.

The bonsai trees' unique presentation and attractiveness has allowed them to spread out from the land of the rising sun and into many countries around the world. Today, bonsai is not something you see just in Japan. In fact, there is even a nonprofit organization called National Bonsai Foundation that showcases bonsai creations of people across the U.S. The foundation is located in northwest Washington D.C., at the US National Arboretum, and its exhibits attract over 200,000 people every year. Some of you might have already heard of the foundation. Others who are new to the world of bonsai might be wondering, "Hold on just a minute. Is bonsai that popular? I thought it would be an activity only a few hundred – maybe a couple of thousand – people would be involved in." Not true at all. You would be surprised at the number of people who are part of the bonsai phenomenon.

Image: A bonsai is a beautiful addition to your home.

Bonsai popularity has reached a level where people have developed their own methods to grow the trees that are slightly different from the Japanese system. This does not mean that the way the trees are grown in Japan is inferior in quality or in approach. Rather, the fact that people have developed their own methods for growing the trees shows a passion for the art of bonsai.

So let's plant our roots into the world of bonsai, raise our crowns of knowledge, and shake our trunks in anticipation (somehow, that last bit didn't come out the way I intended it to).

It is time to plant our understanding with this bonsai care basic guide.

Chapter 1

The History and Tradition of Bonsai

There is certainly more to bonsai than meets the eye. To truly grasp the attention and love that these miniature trees are garnering around the world, it is important to pull back the curtains of history. When we comb through the rich past of bonsai, we begin to uncover a craft that contains an incredible depth to its philosophy. There is so much we can learn about the hobby. To begin with, let's go back to circa 1,000 BC.

A Miniature History Lesson

When people think of bonsai, they often think of Japan. However, some historians believe that the art of miniature tree making had its origins in a much larger country: China. The method of growing trees indoors was perfected by Buddhist monks: their goal was to bring a slice of nature to the indoors. Raising plants was common around the world, which made the monks wonder if there was a way to bring a tree indoors. But if they did, then they wanted to make it small enough to fit inside a room.

When you examine ancient manuscripts and paintings, you can begin to understand the full extent of the passion that the Chinese had for cultivating trees in containers that were "unique" and, most importantly, "artistic."

It is no coincidence that the cultivation of indoor trees first appeared in China. The country is home to a beautiful and diverse flora population. Moreover, many Chinese people had a strong passion for creating gardens in their homes. When they realized that they could add trees to their collection of shrubs and plants, their passion grew even more. They began experimenting with the trees, trying to find the best combinations of plants, flowers, and trees to display. As with many things that are a part of the Chinese culture, the people strove to find a sense of balance. What tree would be perfect in the middle of a garden? How to grow the ideal trees that can adorn the corner of a room?

The Chinese's focus on miniaturization was not merely because of aesthetic reasons. They believed that when objects were smaller, they had a concentrated form of spiritual and mystical powers.

The Japanese started practicing Bonsai during the Kamakura period (between 1185 and 1333) at a time when the practice was also becoming very popular in Asia. As the practice gained popularity, it stopped being something that was just unique to the Buddhist monks and various monasteries. More and more people began using them as a symbol of aristocracy. Growing bonsai was not just a hobby but also a sign of honor and prestige. Over the years however, the philosophy and ideas of bonsai continued to change. Bonsai represents a deep fusion and strong harmony between man, soul and nature among the Japanese. One scroll written during the Kamakura period says that "to appreciate and find pleasure in various curiously curved and potted trees is to really love deformity."

As time went on and bonsai began to spread beyond the borders of Japan, people in other parts of the world more often used it for other purposes. For instance, people presently use bonsai trees for decorative as well as recreational purposes; in this case, the person taking care of the bonsai trees has to take the active role of ensuring that they grow to be beautiful works of art.

The art of bonsai is focused more on beauty rather than production of food or even medicine. You can use almost any tree species to create your own bonsai. However, some trees are much better and easier than others are when it comes to implementing bonsai.

You can see the degree of influence the art of growing miniature trees has on the present world. For example, the creation of Korean and Chinese ceramics has truly amplified the beauty of bonsai. These ceramics were special containers for the bonsai trees. Each ceramic was prepared with great care and attention just like the trees that they held. The Chinese extended the idea of balance to the ceramic as well. They believe that the container and the bonsai tree must become a unified presence. This is why, even though bonsai spread to various parts of Japan, the preferred containers for holding the trees still remain Chinese ceramics.

Image: The Chinese wanted to find a way to bring a tree inside the house.

When the Japanese adopted the bonsai tradition, they added their own styles and interpretations of the art. To this day, there is a marked difference between Chinese and Japanese bonsai styles. Many people consider the Japanese version to be more precise and pleasing. Proponents of the style often consider the Chinese method of raising bonsai trees as crude and unpolished, but in my personal opinion, I think that when you are raising bonsai trees, you use the method that is most comfortable to you. I can provide you a proper guide on raising the trees, but in the end, you will decide what you feel is the best way to create your very own bonsai garden.

Many people ask why the Japanese method of growing bonsai is more popular.

About 800 years ago, the people of Japan were fascinated with various aspects and practices of the Chinese, including Buddhism. When bonsai trees became popular in Japan, almost everyone, from royalty to military personnel to the common folk, would grow a version of the trees in their homes. The royalty, of course, could afford to create works of incredible detail and beauty, while everyday folk would create a much more simplified version of a bonsai tree. But the point remains; there was something meaningful about planting a miniature tree in one's home and watching it grow through careful attention and guidance.

After World War II, Japanese people living in the U.S. popularized bonsai. They began to introduce it in their communities, which eventually trickled down to other communities and before you know it, the bonsai craze had swept the nation.

And of course, there was Karate Kid.

I'm not kidding. Karate Kid offered something to American viewers that other films were not able to do. While the popularity of martial arts movies was not something new, there were barely any movies that popularized them for a mainstream crowd. After Karate Kid was released, entire families were heading to the theater to see a wholesome, family-fun martial arts movie.

But Karate Kid did something more than make martial arts famous: it spread the popularity of bonsai even more. Now everyone wanted to know how they could have their very own miniature tree in their backyard or other space. Gardeners were especially attracted towards bonsai. Since they were already looking for different ways to add color and design to their gardens, the idea of raising a bonsai tree was just too irresistible.

Though, I will have to tell you that it isn't all about just the beauty of the trees. I am not going to say that it isn't the most important aspect about bonsai. It is. The idea of growing a tree and watching it slowly mature into something visually spectacular is a feeling that I can only describe as a combination of awe, pride, and satisfaction. However, there is certainly more to growing bonsais.

The Philosophy Behind Bonsai

When you think of Japan, you are probably going to think of Tokyo, Sakura (cherry blossoms), and Mount Fuji. There is a reason why nature is closely attached to Japanese culture. I mean yes, there is also anime, for you anime-fans. But the point is that when we think of Japan as a country, our minds conjure images of beautiful natural scenes.

Image: The Japanese find ways to appreciate nature.

Nature is part of the Japanese lifestyle as well. From leading an active lifestyle in the midst of nature, to having wholesome food inspired by nature's products, the people of Japan enjoy natural gifts. Just a fun fact, Japan has the highest number of centennials (people who live to the age of 100) than any other country in the world.

This love for nature can be seen in the art of bonsai where the Japanese are able to show their appreciation for trees and display an idea of what they think is beautiful. There is a deep commitment involved in growing trees that is quite different from tending to plants and herbs in a garden. You need to be both physically and emotionally invested to succeed.

But more than that, bonsai fulfils a certain "quest." These days, you can produce bonsai using layering, grafting, or seeding. But when they were first discovered, people had to head into the woods or the forest in order to find the right plant. That plant would then be raised in a careful manner in order to create a beautiful end result. The whole process – from finding the plant to growing the tree – was akin to a journey. A journey that required much patience and care if one were to guide it towards a fruitful conclusion. While today the art of bonsai does not involve a trip to the woods, one still requires patience and putting in the required amount of care into their bonsai tree. Many people consider bonsai as meditative, and they are not too far off the mark.

Growing a bonsai tree is a careful process. You need to pay attention to the tree every day and provide the right amount of sunlight and water. At the same time, you need to carefully trim the plant, check the soil, maintain the overall health of the tree, and perform many other regular tasks. The entire process teaches you to be more patient and careful. You learn to respect the work you put into growing a bonsai and you understand the joy of little things, such as watering the tree or giving it a little trim.

Ultimately, you begin to deeply respect nature, just like the Chinese and the Japanese do. I have seen people who pick up bonsai become deeply troubled by news of deforestation and forest fires. They suddenly expand their admiration for trees and plants to the entire world. Other people have picked up gardening as a hobby to turn a small space into a natural haven. Now I am not saying that everyone who picks up bonsai as a hobby is going to develop the same feelings towards nature. However, I am almost certain that each and every person who starts working on bonsai trees is going to respect living things around them much more deeply.

Traditions

You might think that an art based around raising trees would not have any styles. After all, if we were to grow trees in the wild or in a garden, we wouldn't exactly name their styles of growth. However, bonsai treats things a little differently. We are shaping trees to be similar to the ones we find in the forests or in the woods. As people practiced bonsai over the years, some of the ways to shape trees became more common than others. Those that were popular were given certain names in reference to the way the tree was raised.

Remember that the styles are chosen after decades of work on bonsai. They don't exist merely because they satisfy an aesthetic presentation, although that is equally important as well. The styles are known because they are some of the best ways to grow bonsai. All of the styles have their origins in Japan and form a key part of a long tradition of bonsai tree growing.

Chapter 2

Types of Bonsai Trees

Let's look at the popular styles of growing bonsai. Do note that the English names provided are not official names: they are what the bonsai community uses to refer to the styles.

Popular Bonsai Growing Styles

Moyogi, or "The Curve Style"

In this style, the trunk curves as it grows vertically. This style is fairly common, both in the art of bonsai and in nature as well. Though the tree is upright, the trunk takes on an 'S' shape. In some cases, the trunk takes on a flipped S shape, which gives the impression that you are looking at a reflection of the S shape. Branches grow at every turn or curve of the shape. The trunk is widest at the base and gets progressively narrower as you reach the top.

In this style, the trunk's tapering must be clearly visible and the bottom of the chosen tree should be wider, narrowing upwards to the top.

Ishizuki, or "The Rock Growing Style"

The tree grows on rocks or boulders that have gaps or cracks in them. The roots of the tree have to navigate in the gaps provided by these rocks and the absence of much soil means that they cannot receive the nutrition that they seek. This translates to your plant not having enough room for the development of healthy roots. The absorption of nutrients is also low in this case and this means that the trees will not have a healthy look. This makes it vital for you to water and fertilize often, since the space available is not sufficient to store nutrients and water. Most of the trees that grow in this style do not remain entirely healthy. The trees need constant attention, since they find it challenging to survive without frequent care. Shallow pots are used for this style so that it can hold as much water as possible. Gravel is added to complete the style.

Image: The Moyogi style of growing a bonsai.

Bunjingi, or *"The Literati Style"*

The tree is given the name because of the stylistic nature of the branch, which looks like a calligraphy character. There are no branches on the trunk, save for the ones that form the crown. The pots used to house such trees are round and small.

This style is also present in nature, even though it might seem like something that could only exist in the world of bonsai. A tree adapts this style when it is densely surrounded by many other trees so that the competition for resources, including light, is fierce. The only way for the tree to survive is by growing taller than the other trees surrounding it. The trunk of the tree grows upward, crookedly and only has branching at the crown where the sun can reach. If you want a tree to adopt this style, you need to place it in a small and round pot.

Hokidachi, or "The Upright Broom Style"

In this style, the tree is upright. Branches only begin to grow at a certain height, giving the illusion that the tree has a large crown. Hokidachi style can be best used on deciduous trees that have a fine and extensive branch system. The trunk of the tree goes upright and straight. It does not go all the way to the top of the tree. It goes for about a third of the total height of the tree and then forms branches going toward all directions. The leaves and branches create a crown shaped like a ball. If raised well, then the crown becomes a magical sight to behold, especially during the colder seasons of the year. Some people like to place the tree outside, allowing snow to accumulate on the branches.

Fukinagashi, or "The Windswept Style" or "The Windblown Style"

The trunk of the tree leans on one side, as though it was hit by a strong wind. Typically, the branches of the tree are more or less on one side, though this does not have to be the case with every tree. If you imagine a strong wind pushing the tree and bending it in one direction, then the branches grow on the side not affected by the imaginary wind. In many cases, the branches grow all around the trunk, but eventually bend to grow in the direction that is moving away from the imaginary wind. In nature, the branches start by growing on all sides of the tree but eventually end up bending to one side.

Kengai, or *"The Cascading Style"* or *"The Bent Tree Style"*

The trunk grows until it reaches a certain height and then bends in the opposite direction, growing towards the ground. The result makes it seem like the branches are cascading towards the ground. The shape of the tree makes it look like a crude form of an inverted 'U.' The tree grows in such a manner because it cannot maintain an upright position. Since the trunk begins to extend towards the ground, bonsai in this style are usually planted in tall pots, giving the trunk enough space to grow without actually touching the ground. Many bonsai specialists like to grow the tree slightly horizontally, so that the length of the trunk can extend at a certain height before falling downwards.

You could even think of the growth of the tree as though it was downwards. In nature, this can be because of factors such as falling rocks and snow. Maintaining this growing style can be rather hard, as this direction goes against nature, since trees are supposed to grow upright in normal conditions. Do note that branches should grow on the downward growing trunk, alternating left and right.

Han-kengai, or *"The Semi-Cascading Style"*

This style is similar to the previous style. The only difference is that the trunk does not look like it is moving almost vertically towards the ground. The best way to imagine this style is to think of a slide in a playground. You have the stairs that lead up, which is how the trunk grows upwards. At the top, the slide levels off, and finally, you have the slippery incline angled at almost 45 degrees. That's similar to how trees in this style grow.

This style is found in nature just as the cascade style. The unique aspect of this style as compared to the cascade style is that unlike in cascade style, the trunk in Han-kengai will not grow below the level of the pot. The crown of the bonsai tree will grow above the pot's rim, while the other subsequent branches will grow below the level of the rim of the pot.

Bankan, or "The Coiled Style"

The trunks of this style become twisted and knotted. It looks like the shape a wet cloth makes when you wring it. An important note to be made here is that just because the trunk is twisted, it does not mean that the tree is unhealthy. On the contrary, the tree is quite strong.

Shakan, or "The Slanting Style"

The entire trunk grows at a 70° or 80° angle. It looks like the entire tree is leaning. The strength of the roots differs at the base of the trunk. On the side that is leaning, the roots are stronger, since they have to support the weight of the tree. The roots on the other side are weaker, and mainly hold the tree firmly in place, preventing it from falling entirely.

This style can be formed naturally if a tree grows in a dark place and has to bend towards light, or if the wind constantly blows in one direction: this concept can also be applied to bonsai growing to bend your plant. The only difference is that with the bonsai tree, you should bend it at an angle of approximately sixty to eighty degrees from the ground level. In this style, the roots on one side of the tree are not developed well so the roots on the other side are much stronger and capable of supporting the tree and keeping it standing. The first branch at the bottom should be at the opposite side of the slanting direction to create a visual balance. The trunk can be either straight or slightly bent. The trunk should also be thinner from the bottom upwards.

Chokkan, or "The Typical Upright Style"

This is one of the most popular styles of growing a bonsai tree. The trunk stands in an upright position. Branches shoot away from the trunk at regular intervals. If you spot such a tree in nature, either in the wild or in someone's garden, then it grows with adequate sunlight and nutrition. It is not competing with other trees for resources. You can also have trees that have multiple trunks. These bonsai trees share the same base, or pot.

It does not require a lot of attention to create this style since it only requires a lot of light without any hindrances for your tree to grow upright. In this style, the trunk's tapering must be seen clearly so you should choose a tree that is thicker at the base near the roots and narrows towards the top. The branching should begin at about a quarter of the total height of your tree. The top part (or the crown) of the tree should also be created by one branch, meaning that the trunk will not actually run to the topmost part of the tree.

Netsuranari, or "The Spreading Shape"

In this style, numerous trunks can grow from the same root system. Technically, the entire setup is just one tree, but because one cannot clearly see the roots, it looks like there are several trees growing in the same pot. It should be noted that not all species of trees can grow into this style. There are specific trees that you can use for the purpose, such as the Japanese Cedar or the Needle Juniper.

Ikadabuki, or "The Raft Style"

You are not using the trunk to grow the tree. Instead, you are going to make use of the branches. In some cases, despite a cracked or broken trunk, the branches of the tree can be made to grow. In such cases, the branches are made to point upwards, and the trunk is used as a base. It is like a "raft" that holds the branches up. This style also gives the illusion that there are many trees planted simultaneously. Most people also tend to bury as much of the trunk as possible with soil so that it does not show.

Kadushi, or "The Open Raft Style"

This style is a variation of the previous one. The only difference is in the way the "raft" or trunk is presented. In the previous style, the raft is hidden underneath the soil. That is not the case with this style, where the raft is clearly on display. It does not matter what style you pick, as long as it fits your aesthetic preference. The one point to note here is that people usually prefer to grow an odd number of branches. This is a reflection of the Japanese belief in odd numbers.

It should also be noted that odd numbers attract the eye better. Even though even numbers have a sense of symmetry to them, odd numbered objects build a sense of interest. They force viewers to move their eyes all over the group of objects, allowing them to truly take in the details. In fact, interior stylists and designers prefer odd numbers, since they make the room look better.

Sankan, or "The Fork Style"

Three trunks grow out of the same base. In other words, a tree trunk grows to a certain height and then splits into three smaller trunks. In this style, two of the trunks are larger than the remaining one. The larger trunks are called 'mother' and 'father', while the smaller trunk is called 'son.'

Sokan, or "The Split Style"

This style is similar to the previous style, with the only difference being the fact that the base splits off into two trunks instead of three. In this style, two trunks emerge from the same root system. In other cases, the smaller trunk can grow from the bigger trunk just above the soil. Both trunks will vary in terms of length and thickness. One trunk – the 'father' – is larger than the other – the 'son.' The two trunks form a single crown. This style is more common in nature than it is in the art of bonsai.

Image: The Split Style.

Kabudachi, or "The Multi-Trunk Style"

This style is theoretically like the double trunk style, but with more than two trunks. All the tree trunks grow out of one root system where they all form one canopy. The top part is formed by the most developed and thickest trunk.

Yose-ue, or "The Forest Style"

This style has a similar look as the multi-trunk style. The difference is that the forest style is made up of several independent trees, as opposed to the multi trunk style, which is composed of several trunks of one tree. The trees that are most developed are grown in the middle part of a large pot. Other smaller trees are planted at the sides of the developed one, thus contributing to the formation of a single crown. In this case, the trees are usually not planted following a straight line. Rather, they are arranged in a scattered sequence. This is done to give the miniature forest a more natural and realistic look.

Seki-joju, or "The Growing on a Rock Style"

In nature, this style is common in areas with rocky terrains where the trees growing on the rocks are compelled to look for soil rich in nutrients using their roots. The roots of the plant are unprotected before they penetrate the ground, so the plant adapts by forming a special bark around the roots. In bonsai, the roots of your tree will grow over a rock and into the pot. The most suitable trees for this style are the bonsai ficus and Juniper bonsai.

Bonsai Tradition

The tradition of bonsai revolves around imitating nature. Some people have large containers where they plant several trees, giving the illusion of a forest. Others take the idea one step further by planting trees of different sizes and ages, usually of the same species. The resulting effect is a bonsai composition that looks close to a real forest.

Whether you are focusing your efforts on a single tree or planning to grow multiple trees, the end result is that you are allowing nature to develop inside a small container. It is for this goal to imitate nature that bonsai requires care, attention, and patience.

In fact, those who are aiming to grow a forest should show precise care, because if even a single tree does not grow well, it could ruin the overall visual presentation of the container.

Anatomy of a Bonsai

Understanding the anatomy of a bonsai helps you to work towards creating a tree that has all the visual elements complementing each other.

Pot or Container

Yes. This is an important part of the bonsai experience. The pot or container is a vital part of the tree, since it not only provides a base for the tree to grow from and various nutrients for it, but it is also a powerful visual component.

The shape, size, and the color of the pot should be chosen to match your tree. Here is a simple guideline for when you are trying to choose the size of the pot:

- You should ideally choose a pot where the depth is twice the diameter of the trunk.
- The width of the pot should match the height of the tree or should be one and half times the height.

What about the shape and color? We are going to look at various components that are essential in growing a bonsai in later chapters. Using the recommendations in those chapters, you might get an idea of what kind of tree you would like to pick and how you would like to grow it.

Foliage

Typically, you should pick plants with smaller leaves, since they tend to grow up to become miniature trees. Plants with large leaves do not usually make a convincing bonsai exhibit. If the leaves are large and the rest of the tree is small, then it might give the appearance of a malnourished tree rather than a bonsai presentation. There are also specific techniques, such as pruning, that will help you reduce the size of the leaf.

Branches

Think of the branches as extensions of the trunk. Now that statement might seem rather obvious to you and you might just wonder why I bothered to even mention it. I am not talking in the literal sense. What I am referring to is the aesthetic. If the trunk is straight but the branches are curved or angular, then it creates an odd impression. The branches should extend the visual presentation of the trunk.

Trunk

You have to decide the shape of the trunk before you start working on it. In order to get best results, there should be a lot of "flow" in the trunk. For example, if you have chosen the Moyogi style, then during the first curve, the trunk should move slightly towards the viewer and when the trunk reaches the second curve, it should angle slightly away from the viewer.

However, the most important idea to keep in mind is that you have to ensure there is a balance between the trunk and the branches. As we understood in the previous section, a straight trunk should not have curved branches, and so on.

Try to avoid trunks that may show slight protrusions or bulges in the center. These growths are usually deformities in the tree and are referred to as inverse tapers. If they are allowed to grow, then it becomes a challenge to remove or correct them.

Roots

The roots of your tree usually spread outwards before they dig into the soil. This is how it is with many trees in the wild: some roots are left exposed, while others bury into the ground as soon as they spread away from the trunk. Either way, you should aim to form roots that are solid, since they are a sign of a healthy tree.

When you are able to bring together all the elements of a bonsai, you can create something truly beautiful and healthy.

Chapter 3

Selecting Your Bonsai

If you want to grow a bonsai, the first thing you need is a bonsai. The question is, how can you obtain one, and what are the things that you should consider when making your purchase?

Before we delve into that, I would like to briefly go through the process of growing a bonsai. This process will serve as a guideline for you, and I will explain each segment in detail further in this book.

How Can You Find Your Future Bonsai?

I would like you to first look at various bonsai and study them, before making the actual purchase. If you do not have access to actual bonsai, then try to look at pictures online. The reason I am asking you to do this is so that you can plan things out from a visual perspective. Rather than diving headfirst into raising a bonsai and feeling unsatisfied later (remember, you are going to put time, effort, and emotion into the endeavor), it's better to create an expectation in the beginning.

The best places to find the right bonsai plant is by visiting a plant shop or a local garden. Here is a tip you should remember: always visit those gardens where the bonsai can be seen in the open, preferably in natural light. You will be more likely to end up purchasing good quality bonsai because the garden center is confident about the way they grow their plants and trees. If you visit a florist who places plants and trees under artificial lighting, then there are chances that the lighting itself has been adjusted to make the leaves appear more green than they are. In reality, the person in charge of maintaining the plants might have failed to provide adequate water or taken the plants outdoors for sunlight. Chances are that you might purchase a bonsai that has already suffered a little damage. And yes, there are unscrupulous gardeners who might have used poor soil for the tree.

Image: Think about the kind of bonsai you would like to grow in your house.

To start growing a bonsai tree, the first thing you need to consider is the type of tree that you will use. You should select one that suits the climate of your region. The climate factor can affect the type of tree you will grow greatly since not every species of bonsai tree will work well in all climatic locations. Many of the tropical plants and even woody perennials can be used as bonsai trees. Some trees may die out in freezing conditions while others may actually need freezing weather conditions. This makes it very crucial for you to consider your climate before choosing a tree to plant especially if you are planning on growing an outdoor bonsai tree. If you are unsure of the trees that can survive in your area, you can consult your local farm/garden supply store personnel who will be able to assist you.

As a beginner, you can choose one of the trees mentioned in the *Choosing the Right Style of Bonsai* section in the final chapter of this book. These trees are beginner-friendly. The most recommended tree for you to start with is the juniper. This tree is an evergreen, so it never loses its leaves, and can survive in a variety of weather conditions. Juniper bonsai trees are also very easy to grow and show good response to training efforts such as pruning.

Other types of trees that are most popularly grown as bonsai trees are:

- Conifers such as spruces, cedars, and pines of different varieties
- Deciduous trees (leafy) which include Japanese maples (grown because of their beauty), elms, oaks, and magnolias
- Tropical plants (non-woody) such as snow rose and jade, which are a perfect choice if you wish to plant indoor bonsai in temperate or cool climates.

I would also recommend that you look at your state's agricultural laws. Some states do not allow the importing of plants from other states. Each state has its own laws because of the spread of plant diseases. For example, the law in Texas states that no one can bring in citrus plants, or even parts of the plants, into the state from outside its borders. In order to grow citrus, you will have to acquire the plant from within the state. Of course, one will ever know if you have a citrus plant from outside the state growing in your house. However, it might become apparent if you try to sell citrus products from your bonsai tree, since there is a check made to ascertain the history of the tree and the origin of its purchase.

The Indoor or Outdoor Dilemma

Another important factor to consider when planting your own bonsai is whether you want to plant it indoors or outdoors. The requirements of an indoor tree and an outdoor tree can vary greatly. You must keep in mind that indoor environments receive less natural light and are drier than outdoor environments. If you choose to grow an indoor bonsai, then you will have to choose a tree that requires less moisture and light. Below is a list that shows popular bonsai tree varieties you can grow outside or inside.

Indoor bonsai trees: serissa, Kingsville boxwood, gardenia, cypress, ficus, Hawaiian umbrella and camellia.

Outdoor bonsai trees: cypress, elm, ginkgo, beech, larch, juniper, cedar, birch, and maple.

You should note that some of the hardier bonsai trees, such as the junipers, can be grown in both outdoor and indoor conditions, provided you take proper care of them.

Size Matters

The next step is to choose what size you want your bonsai to grow up to. Bonsai trees can be grown in a number of sizes. For instance, they can be grown to be as little as 15.2 centimeters (six inches) to as tall as about 0.9 meters (3 feet), depending on the type of tree you chose. If you choose to grow your tree from a cutting of another tree or seedling, you can start off your tree even smaller. You should note that larger plants and trees require more soil, sunlight, and water to grow, so you should ensure you supply all the requirements before beginning.

When making a decision on the size of your tree, you should put the following into consideration:

- The presence of sunlight in the area you wish to grow your bonsai tree (whether at home or work)
- The size (width & depth) of the container you will be using
- The space available in the area you wish to plant your bonsai tree in
- Whether you will be able to care for that size of your bonsai tree (bigger trees take much longer before you need to prune them)

If you are planning to get edible bonsai, and by that I do not mean that you can eat the entire tree, but rather what it produces, then you have to check the local climate. Get the opinion of the gardeners and try to understand if the choice of tree is well-suited for the coming months.

Selecting the Pot

Despite the fact that different species might be planted in the same pot size, the plants will differ from each other greatly. Make sure that you also check for diseases and pests before making your purchase. It's important to remember that if you are going to purchase a bonsai from a garden store, they might already be growing in a particular manner, so you won't have full control over the shape it takes. There is an obvious benefit to this. You won't have to worry about shaping the plant from the beginning, like you would with a seedling. The downside is that you have to stick to a predetermined shape. On the other hand, a seedling allows you to start your work from the ground up.

Selecting a pot for your bonsai plant is also necessary because pots can either encourage or restrict growth of the plant. The main feature to look for when choosing the best pot is the size. It should be large enough to allow enough soil that can cover the roots of your plant.

When you water your tree, it absorbs the moisture using its roots. You should therefore ensure that your pot can hold a good amount of soil for your tree, which in turn will allow the roots of your tree to retain moisture. You should ensure that your pot has at least one drainage hole at the bottom. This will help in preventing root rot, which is often caused by too much moisture. If your pot does not have a drainage hole, you can drill some holes yourself.

You should also ensure that your pot is not too large. Very large pots can actually dwarf your tree, leading to a rather odd appearance caused by the imbalance of the size of the pot and the size of the tree. Purchase a pot that is only big enough for the roots of your tree and not any bigger. The main idea here is to bring a visual balance between your pot and tree.

You can also decide to grow your bonsai tree in a separate, plain and practical container then transfer it later into better or more visually striking containers when they are fully grown. This process is useful if you are dealing with a fragile bonsai variety. It actually allows you to skip the part on buying a 'nice' pot until you have a mature, healthy, and beautiful tree.

I strongly recommend that you also maintain good relations with a few garden stores, especially those that are well-stocked or the one you have made your bonsai purchase at. The stores will be able to provide you with expert recommendations and advice if you run into any challenges. Australian cherries, Natal plums, and Dwarf pomegranates are some species of bonsai that are sold as large plants. If you do not want to purchase edible bonsai, then think about the shape of the tree you would like to work on. For example, if you are aiming for the Bankan style, then you are looking to get the Ficus Panda. However, if you prefer the Hokidachi, then the Buxus Bonsai is what you are aiming for. Knowing the shape of bonsai you would like to buy helps you get guidance from the garden store or nursery.

I can also provide you with one final suggestion: keep an open mind. I do understand that you are fascinated by a single style of bonsai, but try to examine all options before you make up your mind.

If you still want to stick to the style you had originally picked, then that means you have made a well-informed choice. You won't have any regrets in the future because you have seen all other options. Alternatively, you might just become fascinated with another style you had never considered before. It's a win-win situation.

Not finding your preferred bonsai or plant in your local garden center? Well, when the real world fails, you turn to the virtual world for assistance. Nearly anything can be found on the internet. All you have to do is boot up your favorite search engine and enter your query. You can always check online stores to get the plants you need. However, make sure that you verify the reputation of the store before you make any purchase. Since you won't be able to see the plant in person, you are placing a lot of trust in the fact that your purchase will arrive in good condition.

I personally found a nice key lime tree online and I was satisfied with my purchase. However, I did research into many online stores before I settled on one that I found trustworthy.

If you prefer to grow your bonsai from its initial stages, then you can use seeds.

Using Seeds to Grow

When you use seeds, then you are making use of the most natural method of propagating. However, I will have to tell you that it might not be the most reliable. And there is the tiny issue of having a whole lot of patience. And I do mean a lot. You will find that this is the case with slow-growing trees. You could start growing some trees when you are in college and it is only after you reach the midpoint of your life that you might finally see the tree taking shape. Some people actually prefer the slow-growing process and if you are one of them, then I cannot recommend seeds enough.

Wild Seeds

If you want to obtain seeds from the wild, then the best time to look for them is during fall. Using a little observation and a small degree of skill, you will be able to find all kinds of seeds to work with. But you might also face the problem of trying to identify what tree the seed belongs to. Unless you have knowledge about the seeds in the area you are searching, you won't be able to accurately identify the seeds. Certain seeds are quite distinguishable, such as chestnuts or acorns. However, you might face a challenge if you come across numerous species of conifers all growing in the same area. In that case, you might hold up a seed and wonder if it belongs to pine or juniper. Perhaps a cedar? It could also be a cypress.

Let's say that you managed to identify the seeds, the chances of successfully growing a tree from a seed that you find in the wild or among nature are really slim. You may find certain seeds attacked by fungal or viral diseases, while others have been affected by parasites. You don't often find seeds that are clean and healthy in the wild.

However, while it is my responsibility to make you aware of the many challenges you might face when using seeds in the wild, I will not discourage you entirely. There is a certain joy in heading out into the wild and finding a seed and then transforming that seed into a tree, despite how long it could take.

This brings us to another option for obtaining seeds.

Commercial Seeds

If you still prefer using seeds, then I can recommend buying them from stores. These seeds are free of any diseases or parasites.

A final point to remember is that no seed will automatically grow into a bonsai. Trees are naturally large and the seeds will reflect that. You need to provide care and attention in order to ensure that you get the size you were looking for.

I would also recommend not entirely trusting the image that you see on seed packets. They do not always indicate what the final result will be. I have seen people who were expecting to mimic the tree in the picture, only to end up feeling entirely disappointed in their results. Each seed is unique. Despite all your best efforts, you may never replicate the results of another specimen down to the last detail.

Planting Seeds

Always ensure that you have good quality seeds before you begin. If you are growing seeds in fall (which should be around the time you collect them), then you can begin immediately. However, if you come across seeds that need to be sown in spring, then make sure that you place the seeds in an airtight container, preferably in a cool place. You can refrigerate the seed if there isn't a cool spot in the house.

You can then choose to grow the tree in soil prepared for the purpose, inside a container, or in a pot. Before the seed is planted, it is often soaked for a day in lukewarm water. If the seed has a thick outer layer, then you might need to make a small incision on the surface, without affecting the seed inside. In case you are unsure of how to do it, then you can always visit the local garden store for help. If the seed has a hard shell protecting it, then you might have to crack it open carefully.

Whether you are cracking open the seed or making an incision on it, you need to first soak the seed. This ensures that the outer layer becomes soft and easy for other processes.

Some seeds might require you to subject them to an additional process known as stratifying. The Gray Bark Elm and Japanese White Pine are examples of such seeds.

Stratification of Seeds

Step 1

Take out a mixing bowl and add about ¼ cup of sand.

Step 2

Start adding water slowly until the sand reaches a density where you can easily form balls with it.

Step 3

When the sand is ready, add the preferred seed variety into it in the amount that you require.

Step 4

Transfer the soil along with the seed(s) into a ziploc bag.

Step 5

Place the ziplock bag in the refrigerator for about a month. If you notice the seeds begin to sprout plants before the end of one month, then take them out immediately and transfer them into the soil prepared for growing them.

TIP

If you prefer, you can replace sand with peat moss, which is easier to find in certain areas. The steps you have to follow when using peat moss is the same as the ones you follow for sand.

Sowing the Seed

For the majority of the seeds you come across, you might be using a soil that is a mixture of sand, loam or clay, and peat. You might have to make adjustments in the ratio of the three kinds of soil. However, I would like you to get all the details about your seed. There are instances in which you might require an acidic soil instead: in that case, you might have to use only peat. Sometimes, you might not have to use peat at all.

Regardless of what soil composition you end up using, you need to remove debris, large materials like pebbles, and any other impurities that you may find. I also recommend getting a garden sieve. Make sure that you use a fine meshed sieve for the soil that will cover the seeds.

Understanding Containers

Many people are not aware of this and are left unprepared when the plant begins to grow. When you notice the first leaves on the seedling, then you are most likely going to repot it several times. While repotting is usually the norm, it is not mandatory. It depends on the seeds that you use. Be aware of the fact that the container or pot that you use in the beginning might not be the pot that you use later.

The final tray is the one that you will use to house the bonsai.

Image: A small gap at the bottom along with holes which allow for proper drainage.

Regardless of what container you use in the beginning, make sure that it features a drainage hole, preferably at the bottom, in order to remove excess water. Why is excess water harmful? It can drown the seeds. That's right. People have this idea that the more water they add, then the healthier the seed grows up to become. But more is not always merrier.

Also ensure that the base of the container has sand or gravel in order to support water drainage. You might also have to make use of potting compost. Find out the kinds of composts that are sold in your local garden store and get to know more about them. Always ask for assistance if you are uncertain about what compost you should be getting.

Run the compost through a sieve to remove any thick clumps. Remember that the larger the seed, the most compost you might have to use. Large seeds need a covering of 1 to 2 cm of compost. For small seeds, you only need to dust a layer of compost on top of them. If the seeds are tiny, then it is recommended that you avoid using compost, since it can prevent the seed from even sprouting.

Gently run a spade or any other tool with a flat surface over the compost after adding it, but make sure that you do not press down on the soil too much. When you have 'flattened' the soil, it is time to water it for the first time. If you are using small seeds and you have only dusted a layer of compost, then use a sprayer to spray a thin mist of water.

But what about seeds that are left uncovered? Use this trick for such seeds. Take a wide container filled with water. Transfer the pot (ensuring that it has an opening at the bottom) into the container filled with water. This allows the soil to absorb the water from the bottom. This process could push out the tiny seeds at the top, so make sure that you keep an eye out for the seeds.

Initially, avoid placing the seedling in direct sunlight, or you might risk causing dehydration. Make sure that it receives adequate water, but do not flood the pot as this could cause fungal infection. When the seedling becomes a plant, you can transfer it to a clay pot. At this time, you can also provide nutrition to the plant in the form of fertilizers.

When the plant enters the second year since you started germinating it, you can begin the bonsai process. However, it does not mean that you can transfer the plant to a bonsai container or tray. You might have to wait until the third year for that.

Plant Propagation

The term propagation is used to describe a process in which the plant is grown using methods other than the planting of seed in a soil. Depending on the plant, you might have to apply one of many propagation methods.

Layering

The simplest form of layering is done by bending the branch of a small tree or a large plant to the ground. It would be ideal if you used the lowest branch on the trunk or a low-hanging branch. Bring the tip of the branch to the ground and cover it with soil. Do not bury the branch deeply: you should cover it with enough earth to keep it anchored. Next, you have to encourage the process of rooting. To do this, score the bark of the branch lightly (the part that is buried in the ground). Then add rooting powder into the burial spot. The roots mostly appear during spring. In most cases, you can separate the new plant layer from its parent branch during fall. However, just to be on the safe side, wait until winter before you sever the connection.

I can guess what you are thinking. Just how does it work in a pot? Simple. Typically, you bend the branch until it reaches the ground. When you have a pot, you bend the branch until it reaches the pot soil. Then you simply have to proceed as per the instructions provided above.

Cutting

With this method, you take a small portion of a living tree, preferably a twig or a stem, and allow that portion to grow roots. The simplest method is to simply place the twig in a glass of water. However, this may not work with all tree species. Twigs from succulents can be dipped in water until the roots start to take form. Then it is simply a matter of transferring that twig into a pot.

Alternatively, you can dip the base of the twig in hormone powder. Make sure that you remove excess powder by gently shaking the twig. If there are leaves on the twigs, then only keep those on the upper portion of the twig (or the part of the twig that is going to be above the soil). You can cut the remaining leaves, but ensure that the buds are left intact at the axils. As for the pot, you should ideally aim to get a clay pot. Add sand mixed with peat. Water the plant well. I recommend using the method that was used for watering tiny seeds; allow the soil to suck the water from a container. Make a tiny hole at the top and insert the portion of the tree into it gently. If you do not make a hole, then the surface of the soil will remove the hormone powder at the bottom of the twig. Use your fingers to firmly secure the twig.

Most beginners water the plant from a container. But here is an expert tip: make use of a sprayer and mist the stem.

Chapter 4

Care Guide for Your Bonsai

I have repeated this throughout the book but it begs another mention: a bonsai requires proper and careful care. So how can you care for your bonsai?

The first thing to remember is that you should not get into bonsai if you are not able to allot a certain time everyday to take care of the tree. You need to regularly groom, ensure the tree is in good health, and clip any unnecessary parts out.

You can't simply grow it to a certain point and leave it at that, hoping that the tree will grow up to be healthy on its own. Usually, if left to grow on their own, bonsai never grow up into a healthy and good looking tree. They aren't like other potted plants.

So what do we need to do to ensure that the bonsai grow properly?

Feeding

People in the bonsai community are not open to the idea of using synthetic fertilizers on their plants. The main reason for this is that synthetic fertilizers go against the natural approach of bonsai. There is a deep respect for the gifts of nature, and anything artificial makes people growing bonsai feel as though they are not following the traditions established by centuries of bonsai cultivators.

The primary requirements for healthy and beautiful bonsai are sunlight and adequate (and not too much) water, but in order to bring out the full beauty of the tree, you need to pay attention to your choice of fertilizer as well.

Many bonsai enthusiasts often ask the question; why fertilizers? Bonsai are not like trees in the wild, which are large and have an intricate root system, and this is primarily the reason why bonsai needs fertilizers. They are usually placed in pots and that means they don't have a lot of room to spread their roots for nutrients. Plus, the soil they are in does not have enough nutrients either. Trees in the wild have the freedom to dig their roots deep in search of nutrition.

When it comes to fertilizers, most of the ones that you can get at your local garden store or nursery feature three vital ingredients:

- Nitrogen (N)
- Phosphorus (P)
- Potassium (K)

When buying fertilizers, the packaging or container comes with an NPK value. The value lets you know what amount of the total fertilizer is taken up by each of the aforementioned ingredients.

You may usually see the value represented in three numbers. For example, if the fertilizer shows 16-16-16 on it, then you have to conclude the below:

- Nitrogen - 16%
- Phosphorus - 16%
- Potassium 16%

In a similar manner, a 25-4-2 fertilizer can easily let you know what percentage of each ingredient you can find in it. If one or two ingredients are missing, then the value is represented by a zero. For example, a fertilizer with 12-0-0 has no phosphorus or potassium.

Each of the ingredients in a fertilizer has its own important role to play. Nitrogen assists the bonsais in producing lush, green leaves and strengthening their stems. Phosphorus goes to work on the root system, keeping the roots healthy and allowing them to become used to various training processes and styling techniques without suffering too much damage. If you are producing flowers and fruits, then you might need potassium to ensure abundant produce. The kind of fertilizer you want depends on the bonsai you are growing.

You can use fertilizers that have 14-14-14 nutrient content in them. The bonsai fertilizer from Super Bonsai is one such example. It is recommended that you consult with the local nursery or garden center to understand what kind of fertilizers they have and what you might need.

It is important to note you should only attempt to feed bonsai that are healthy. These bonsai do not suffer from any illnesses or stress-induced side effects. Using fertilizer on bonsai in poor health won't change their condition. In fact, sick bonsai find it difficult to use the nutrients provided to them. This does not mean that sick bonsai cannot grow healthy again. However, it is best to allow them to recover on their own before attempting to feed them any nutrients.

Here are a few more points that you should know about fertilizers:

They do not assist the growth of the bonsai. Rather, they are used to ensure the survival of the tree and prevent the bonsai from becoming sick or weak.

Many people might claim to know the exact way to use fertilizer. In reality, there are no precise measurements for usage. Most of the time, you are given a set of guidelines, which you should use based on your best judgment and analysis of the tree.

Too much is not always a good thing. Some gardeners think that adding a little extra fertilizer will ensure that the tree or plant has enough to last for a little while longer and prefer adding more in the hope that they won't have to check the tree as frequently. While I understand their strategy, I don't recommend or endorse it. In fact, I must frown upon their lack of understanding of fertilizer usage. You see, too much can be a bad thing. Here are a couple of reasons why:

- You are essentially trying to create a dwarf tree, and adding extra fertilizer to such a tree might lead to 'overfeeding.' Think of it like sitting at a long dinner table that's filled with all kinds of food. It would take you an entire month to finish all of that food. What would happen if you tried to stuff yourself as much as possible over the course of just one evening? Not a good feeling is it? A similar situation applies to trees as well.

- Another side effect of adding too much fertilizer is that it could cause the roots to 'burn.' This kills the root and eventually kills the plant or tree.

Keep in mind the important tips below about fertilizer use. For non-flowering trees, add fertilizer anywhere from spring to autumn.

- When it comes to flowering plants, do not add any fertilizer until you begin to see the flowers themselves. This goes for fruit trees as well.
- If you are raising deciduous trees, then ensure that you do not stop feeding until you spot leaves dropping. This helps the tree to replace lost leaves with healthy ones.
- Some fertilizers come in pellet form. When using these, allow them to be completely absorbed by the tree before you add new pellets. If you add more, then you are going to overfeed the tree, which is something that we want to avoid.
- If it is winter, don't bother using fertilizers. I came across a few gardeners who panicked about the fact that the trees had no fertilizers. They began to wonder if the cold would affect tree health and if they should simply just give nutrients, in case the trees need them. Here is a fact; plants and trees do not take in a lot of nutrients during winter. What they need most is the right amount of sunlight and water.
- Do not compare bonsai to other forms of potted plants. You might think that I have just made an obvious statement. However, too many people forget the difference when shopping for fertilizer. They wonder what harm there could be when using fertilizer meant for plants on bonsai. It's the same concept, right? Wrong. Use bonsai specific fertilizers or choose organic fertilizers.
- For all indoor bonsai, do not provide any nutrients to them for at least three months after you have re-potted them. Growing bonsai is a patient process. There is no need to rush things.

Placement

Water, sun, air, and temperature make the world go round. Well, at least they do for bonsai. I know that it is tempting to think of bonsai as plants, but they are trees. And if you notice any tree in the wild, then it has access to adequate water (in the form of rain), sun, and the right air and temperature.

When your bonsai grows up to become something beautiful, you may feel inclined to place the tree in the house, and then call the entire neighborhood to come check out the bonsai. But I say to thee, resist such temptation. Keeping bonsai indoors is not going to help them grow. In fact, you might just destroy their health permanently.

For each season, here is the breakdown of how long you can keep the bonsai inside your home.

- Winter: one or two times a week, not longer than two or three hours.
- Spring: one or two times a week, not longer than two or three hours.
- Fall: one or two times a week, not longer than two or three hours.
- Summer: Never bring the bonsai inside the house, unless there is proper ventilation. What exactly do I mean by proper ventilation? Well, there shouldn't be a huge difference between the outdoor areas and the indoor areas. The amount of air and the levels of temperature should be more or less the same.

However, I understand that people would like to have a tree inside the house. What could be the solution? Tear down the roof? Let's not take drastic measures. Bring the sun into your home by careful placement of mirrors? We are talking about growing bonsai, not putting out a trap for Indiana Jones.

Image: Your bonsai needs to be placed in an area that receives proper sunlight.

Well, there is one solution; grow more bonsai. When you have multiple bonsai, then you can place them inside your house on rotation. There are two ways to do this:

- You can grow the same tree multiple times. This is probably the easier method since you can use the same techniques of training and growing for all the trees. You can place a tree for two to three hours inside your home and then take it back outside to replace it with another tree. You may not be able to do this constantly, unless you have a large collection of trees, but it will help you scratch that indoor decor itch.

- The other method is to use different tree species. They add unique colors and aesthetics to your interiors. They create unique scenes and you might not use the same tree consecutively. However, raising different species of trees means that you have to pay extra attention to them. Each tree might require unique attention.

Regardless of what option you choose, I should warn you that growing multiple bonsais is not recommended for beginners. I strongly suggest that you work on one tree and learn to become comfortable with the bonsai process before moving on to other trees.

Many bonsai veterans will tell you that it takes years to figure out how to water a bonsai properly. They are not entirely wrong. I have personally seen people choose to ignore watering guidelines and do what they felt was right at that time. Keep in mind the below rules:

- Rain, well, or spring water is the best source of water for bonsai. If you do not have access to any of these sources, then use tap water placed inside an open container. Keep the container outside for about 24 hours before you use them on the tree.
- You should ideally be using a sprayer to mist the plants. However, one can also make use of a watering can, especially those that have a long spout. When using the can, keep the opening of the spout above the soil. When pouring the water, use up and down movements to simulate rain conditions.
- The amount of water that you need to use for each tree will vary. Make the best decision based on the weather, soil conditions, and of course, the tree species. However, if you have planted the tree in rocks, then the trees are going to need constant perspiration.
- In the off-chance that the pot has become extremely dry, you might notice the leaves starting to droop, as though they

have become exhausted. Some of them might dry up entirely. When you notice these signs, do not water the tree immediately. It's time for damage control. Take the plant indoors. Use a syringe to spray water on the plants. During the evenings, when there is no sun, you can take the pot back outside. Start by spraying a little water. The next morning, before the sun rises, bring the pot back inside and increase the amount of water you spray. Continue the process for three days. The most important thing to remember is that the pot should be kept in the shade, away from direct sunlight.

Spraying

Ideally, when you water the soil, you should also spray the leaves separately. When the temperature outside is hot or if it is summer, then spray the water just after dawn (anytime between 7 to 8 AM) or a little before dusk (anytime between 4 to 5 PM).

As mentioned earlier, give a quick mist for the leaves. Don't spray so much that it looks like the leaves are drowning in water.

Repotting

Many people have asked me over the years; why does one have to use multiple pots? Why can't everyone just use a large pot? Wouldn't it save time and effort? Not to mention, you can just grow the tree in the same pot until it is time to transfer the tree to a beautiful tray.

There are a few reasons:
- When you use a big pot, the plants will use the nutrition you provide them and their energy reserves in growing the root. They do not spend enough energy on growing the foliage or in the flowering process. This means that even after years,

you are going to wonder why your tree isn't growing as well as it should, why there aren't enough leaves, or for that matter, why there is an abundance of unhealthy leaves.
- Also, it is difficult to maintain water level of the soil. When the pot is big, you have to add enough water to reach the roots. Since the soil will absorb and drain the water, you need to add enough for the tree. A lot of the time you might just end up adding so much that the roots might begin to drown.
- Let's not forget the fertilizer levels. Bigger soil content means more fertilizer, but that does not necessarily spell good news for the tree itself.

People told me that repotting is too much added effort. However, the whole process of bonsai involves a lot of work. You can also make use of specialized bonsai trays. To be clear, these are not the containers that will house the final version of your tree. Rather, these trays are specifically used for growing the tree. They come with holes at the bottom so they can facilitate many watering methods.

Image: Repotting is important to maintain the health of the roots.

How to Remove the Bonsai from the Pot?

When it is time to transfer the bonsai from one pot to another, you have to be careful when removing the plant or tree. You should begin by not watering the soil. Eventually, you will notice the compost turn dry. When the compost is fairly dry, then grab the trunk and pull gently. The plant should come out of the pot easily. If it doesn't, then the compost isn't dry enough.

At this point, you might be faced with a challenge. You need to dry the compost further, but at the same time, you need to keep the bonsai healthy. That means adding water, but not too much of it to make the compost too wet.

Soil Checkup

It is important to check the health of the soil before deciding to repot the bonsai. The most important things that you have to check for are creatures that are not supposed to be there, such as insect larvae, woodlice, or ants. You should also be able to keep track of the development of the root before you can even think about repotting the plant.

In order to deal with insects and diseases, I am going to provide recommendations further in the book. But for now, just know that examining your bonsai is extremely important before you try to do anything.

Cleaning Roots

Start by removing your plant from its current container or pot carefully to avoid tearing or breaking its main stem. You can use a potting shovel to pry out the plant. Most of the roots are going to be cut prior to repotting it, so you have to clean the roots by brushing off any dirt stuck on them. You can use tweezers, chopsticks, root rakes or any other tools of the sort to do this. You don't have to clean the roots until they are spotless. Just clean them enough to be able to see them during pruning.

Pruning the Roots

When you are repotting the plant, you should also think about pruning the roots. After pulling the bonsai from the plant, use a bonsai rake to gently scrape away any excess soil. You will also be able to remove any tangle in the roots through this process. The key word here is 'gently,' because any excess pressure to the roots could destroy them permanently.

Now use scissors with a wide handle but a small blade in order to carefully snip at the roots. You should cut the roots to half their length. However, if you notice roots that are unhealthy or have suffered damage, then simply snip away as much of the root as possible. I have noticed a few gardeners try to tug at the roots in order to remove them. Avoid doing that. You might damage the tree entirely.

Since you should prune the roots at the beginning of spring, I would also recommend repotting at the same time. To successfully repot your bonsai during spring, make sure you are keeping a careful eye on the growth of the plant. If you think that the following spring is a good time for repotting, then go ahead and get ready to remove the plant from its old pot. Don't try to wait for a later date, thinking that perhaps you could wait another year before repotting the plant.

Also remember that I recommend the ideal time for repotting the plant. You can repot it anytime you like, but just make sure you are sure of your actions and are prepared to take care of the bonsai after it has been repotted.

Important Point to Note About Pruning

If the growth of the roots of your bonsai tree is not controlled adequately, the roots may actually outgrow its container. To make sure that your tree stays tidy and manageable, prune the roots before potting it. Cut off any thick, upward-facing, and large roots to leave a network of slender and long roots that will be close to the surface of the soil. Water is actually absorbed by the tips of roots, so many thin strands of roots would be better in a small container rather than a deep, thick one.

The Repotting Process

Choose a pot of the right size. After that, make sure that you use a sieve for each layer you add. The bottom later should be made of gravel or sand in order to facilitate proper drainage. Once you have added the bottom layer, then you have to add the right compost and soil type, based on the tree you are growing.

I recommend getting a bonsai tray for another reason. Or you could use a pot with multiple holes. There could be some difficulty keeping the tree in an upright position and some gardeners use stakes to secure the tree, but that is a bad idea. In order to use a stake well, you must drive it through the base of the tree, potentially harming the roots in the process. I won't say that this method does not work at all, but I don't recommend it for beginners. One needs great experience with trees to drive a stake through them properly. What you try instead is run wires over the base of the tree and through the holes. If you are wondering what 'base' I am talking about, it is the one that is still attached to your tree after you pull it from its previous pot. When removing a tree, you don't just remove the roots. There will be a thick clump of soil still attached to the tree. I don't recommend that you remove this base. If you still want to remove it, then wait till you repot the tree and then carefully scrape it off using a bonsai rake. I would wait until you are able to secure the tree in the new pot properly before trying to remove anything.

Keep in mind that you have to remove the wires after the roots begin to extend into the soil and the tree is able to support itself in the new pot. Once you have added in the necessary compost and other soil components, you can use a spatula to even the top layer. Just remember to not use the spatula for your food ever again.

At this point, I recommend placing a small shelf or cabinet outdoors that will house all your bonsai equipment. If you are keeping the tools inside the house, make sure that you wash them thoroughly and dip them in alcohol solution before storing them.

Once you have repotted the plant, begin by watering it. You should water the plant slowly until you start to notice excess water running out of the pot or container. This process might take a fair bit of time, since you are watering a bigger pot and the compost is dry.

I would also place the bonsai in a shaded area so that the water content does not evaporate quickly.

A final word of advice: always confirm the kind of pot you are going to use for repotting in advance. If you shift the tree from one pot to another and end up changing your mind, then you might be able to correct your action without causing harm to the tree.

Important Note About Repotting

Before you place your tree in the pot, make sure you put some new and fresh soil at the base. At the bottom of the pot, you can add in a layer of a little coarse grained soil to act as the base. On top of that layer, add a looser and finer soil. Make sure the soil you use has the ability to drain well (regular garden soil may retain too much water which may drown your tree). Finally, leave a small space at the top part of the pot as an allowance to cover the roots of your tree.

Repotting Entire Bonsai Trees

If you are purchasing an entire bonsai tree, in most cases you might have to repot it since it may come in a plastic container, and those are not really appealing. Before you go on to pot your plant, you need to prepare it.

First, ensure that you have pruned your tree to your desired shape. If you would also like to style or train your tree before potting it, you can use either of the two common training techniques; wiring or pruning, which will be discussed later.

Most of the trees that have life cycles also follow certain seasons. This is fairly common in a variety of deciduous trees, which are best repotted during spring. Why specifically spring? It is because the rise in temperatures during spring may cause most of the plants of the trees to have an increase in growth, which will assist in quick recovery from root trimming and pruning.

You should also reduce watering the day before you are supposed to repot, since loose and dry soil can be a lot easier to work with as opposed to damp soil.

Important Point About Repotting

Position your tree in the pot you prepared in the step above. Now you can fill the space you left out with the well draining and fine-grained soil, ensuring you completely cover the root system of your tree. If you want to enhance the look of your tree, you can opt to add a top layer of gravel or moss.

If you notice that your tree is bending to one side, and you want to make it more stable, put a heavy gauge wire to run from the pot's bottom, through the drainage holes to the roots of your tree. Tie that wire around the roots to hold your plant in place.

To avoid soil erosion from your pot through the drainage holes, you can mesh screen over the holes.

Initial Care for Repotted Bonsai

The process of repotting and pruning the tree is, in some ways, traumatic to the plant. For about two to three weeks after the repotting, you should leave the tree in an area with a semi shade, free from wind and direct, harsh sunlight. Water the plant, but do not use any fertilizer until roots have grown and become well established. By doing this, you will be giving time for your plant to recover and adapt to its new environment.

For deciduous trees, you should repot them during spring due to their yearly life cycles. This is because they often experience rapid growth during spring. After repotting an indoor deciduous tree and giving it time to take root, you can move it outside with the goal of triggering its inbuilt 'growth spurt' mechanism. The mechanism becomes active in the presence of increased sunlight and rising temperatures. To make your bonsai tree more visually stunning, you can add onto its pot other smaller plants which should be maintained and arranged carefully. To do this, use plants with the same origin as the bonsai tree.

Watering

Water is an essential part of life, both for us humans and for every living creature on this planet. In a natural setting, a tree that requires more water extends its roots deeper into the earth. This allows it to look for moisture underground. In a pot, there are no natural reserves of water for it, so you have to manually supply the container with moisture.

When it comes to bonsai, the amount of water you need to provide for it depends on the size of the tree. Even if your area receives sufficient rain and you place the bonsai outdoors, it does not mean that you can stop watering the plant entirely.

If you have a single bonsai, then you can use watering cans for the soil and sprayers for the leaves, as mentioned earlier. However, if you are growing multiple bonsai, then using a water can is not going to be the easiest method to water all the plants. It might take you a really long time. There are two options. The first is that you concentrate on one bonsai. Learn to understand how to train and raise one bonsai first. If you are growing multiple bonsai, you can use a sprinkler system. Your sprinkler device should not be placed on the ground but above the pots. This way, every time you water the plants, you are stimulating rainfall. Additionally, by using sprinklers, you are both providing water to the soil and misting the leaves.

Most people have trouble figuring out a proper watering schedule. The general rule of thumb is that you should ensure the compost is moist. Do not allow the soil to become dry and prevent it from becoming waterlogged. You should aim to water frequently, but in small quantities.

Image: A watering can simulates the effects of rain.

If you have pruned the roots of the bonsai, then avoid watering too much for a few weeks. But after that, continue to water the bonsai based on the recommendations provided above. When using the watering suggestions provided here, also note the amount of rainfall your area receives. Sometimes, excessive rain can also be damaging. If there are frequent days of heavy rainfall, then keep the bonsai in a shade and water it using the can and sprayer.

Some people also place their trays or pots at an angle in order to drain excess water. This is not a bad recommendation, but I would advise you to be careful, since the angle of the tray could affect the growth of the tree. If you are aiming for a particular shape, then the tree could end up leaning to one side, the branches might droop lower than necessary or the root system might grow well on one side but poorly on the other.

If you have indoor bonsai, then you won't face a lot of trouble with excess rainfall and waterlogging, but that does not mean that you can relax entirely. Bonsai is a complicated process and you need to give proper attention to your trees.

Long-Term Bonsai Care

I have seen people look at pictures or watch videos of beautifully grown bonsai and try to imitate the style without understanding all the efforts they have to put into training and growing the plant. They don't realize that the owners of the bonsai they saw have maintained and raised the trees in the ideal environment, and that environment plays an important role in the health of the bonsai. For example, when someone picks a place in their home to display the bonsai, that place may not necessarily be the right environment for growth. Since we are on the topic of indoor conditions, let me mention a few important guidelines that you need to be aware of.

One of the critical – and I think it just might be the most critical – factors to maintain in indoor conditions is lighting. Some people are able to get or build a greenhouse, which provides the best conditions for bonsai. However, most people cannot simply build a greenhouse. Ideally, you should have sufficient sunlight in the room. For best results, place the bonsai close to the windows. Again, as you provide sunlight to the tree, don't assume that just because the bonsai is indoors, it does not require the same amount of attention it received when it was outside. You still need to water the plant using the same schedule that you would've used in an outdoor setting. Many bonsai trees will automatically move their branches so that their leaves can take in the most sunlight. If you allow them to remain in such a position for long, then they might assume that position permanently. You can of course correct the position, but it will take a bit of effort from your end. The easiest way to correct the position is by rotating the plant every day. If your tree has already matured, then you won't have much problem with the branches trying to move in a particular direction, since they will most probably be strong and sturdy by then.

However, certain bonsai, such as citrus for example, can extend their branches out to get more sunlight. You could think about installing artificial lighting inside your home. Many people prefer to have tube lighting. I have seen some people actually convert the lighting in one whole room to use tube lighting. I would personally recommend against using tubes. There are two reasons for this:

- You might get lighting that is too weak for a tree. Tube lighting works well for seedlings, but doesn't have the same effect on full-grown bonsai trees.
- If you can get tube lighting with enough power for a bonsai, the drawback is that this kind of lighting consumes much energy and is very expensive. Also, if you install them in a room or dedicated area, it is not recommended for you to stay there long since the lighting can be harmful to your skin.

I recommend using a plant bulb that lights a small spotlight. The lighting is more focused and you can direct it specifically to the leaves of the tree. Lighting fixtures can also be placed anywhere from four to ten feet away from the plant depending on the kind of bulb.

Soil

When it comes to the choice of soil and its conditions, I highly recommend that you use the right soil for the kind of bonsai you are growing. However, I can understand how people might not have access to all the required materials. If you feel that you cannot get your hands on soil for bonsai, then you are free to use soil used for potting houseplants. Remember that houseplant soils are not very acidic. In order to increase their acidity, you can use peat moss, if available, or acid fertilizers, which are easier to get.

It is also important to get your repotting schedule right. Bonsai that grow slowly can go up to two years without the need for repotting. As they grow older, you might have to repot them even more rarely. Bonsai that grow quickly might need frequent repotting.

Pot

If you are planting bonsai that give the impression that there are multiple trees in the pot, do not hesitate to use large pots when the bonsai grow out of the seedling stage. This is especially true if you are trying to grow bonsai that produce fruits. But this comes with a caveat. If you use big pots when they are growing, then you will have a difficult time transferring the tree to a bonsai container, since the root system will have extended so far deep that even pruning them will take a lot of time and might not give you the results you seek. I still want to mention the possibility of using large pots so that you have the option.

When potting, you can also add a random arrangement of rocks on the surface. Don't add too much or you won't be able to water the soil properly. And remember, odd numbers are the way to go.

Bonsai Damage

There are various ways in which your bonsai can get damaged, but assuming that you have been taking care of your bonsai, the three most common damages that could befall a bonsai are below:

Leaf Bud Damage

Sometimes, you might notice brown or shriveled leaf buds, especially new ones. This could happen because of several reasons:

- A drastic change in the temperature. Changes in temperature could happen if you keep the bonsai in a warm room and transfer it to a cold area outside in the evening. This problem can be addressed by finding a nice, protected area such as the inside of a garage or a shed. I recommend another location instead of keeping the tree always indoors in your home because if you use the air conditioner or other means to keep the house cool at night, it can eventually damage the bonsai.
- Some leaves can become fairly tender. The sunlight they receive might be too strong for them. Tender leaves are formed when the tree has been placed away from direct sunlight for a long time and then reintroduced to the outdoors. A simple solution to this problem is to provide adequate sunlight to the bonsai whenever possible. This way, your tree does not become sunlight-deprived.

- Strong winds can cause considerable damage to the leaf buds since they are too small to protect themselves. To protect against strong winds, you can bring the tree indoors or create a makeshift shelter. If you have a greenhouse, that would be ideal for your bonsai, since you can provide it with adequate sunlight even during windy weather.
- Contact with furniture or other parts of the house. In the process of moving the bonsai between indoors and outdoors, newly-formed buds may come in contact with hard surfaces. It takes just a light nudge to damage the buds, so always be careful when transporting the bonsai.
- Buds can be damaged by insects. I am going to talk about disease and insect protection further in chapter six.
- Dehydration. Refer to the information I shared about watering to understand how best to keep your bonsai moist.

Leaf Damage

Some of the common reasons why leaves could suffer damage are:
- If the buds receive damage, the resulting leaves that grow are not going to be healthy. Protect the buds using the methods presented in the previous section.
- If the roots are unhealthy or damaged, this can affect the leaves as well. Adding too much or too little water does not merely affect the root system, but it has an impact on the leaves too. After all, the roots transport water and nutrients from the soil to the trunk and leaves.
- If you subject your bonsai to long periods of rain and then provide them with sunlight. This does not improve their condition but worsens it. When your bonsai has aged into a strong tree, you won't have this problem as much. However, if the bonsai is young – and by that, I mean a seedling – then the sudden shifts in temperature could harm the leaves.

- Strong winds must be avoided. They can cause the leaves to shrivel. Like with the buds, provide shade or protected space.
- The temperature of the water spray you use. If you have subjected your bonsai to sunlight, then don't spray them with cold water. The temperature change can be quite a shock to the leaves and they shrivel up.
- If you have pets in the house, then do not allow them to urinate into the pot. I once knew a gardener who allowed his pet dog to poop into the pot, thinking that it could be a replacement for 'organic manure.' Please do not attempt anything like that. Because if plants had the ability to talk, then they wouldn't be praising that gardener's name.

Branch Damage

There are many ways to evaluate branch damage. If you notice the branch slowly dying, that is a surefire indication of a disease. If that is the case, then you will need to identify the disease and treat it. I am going to give you a rundown on some of the common diseases that might affect a plant and how you can deal with them in chapter six.

Image: Depending on your bonsai, it might not be easy to spot branch damage.

Whatever the reason for the damage, the best plan is to ideally snip off the branch and treat it as mentioned in the section on pruning. A lot of people have asked me why treat the tree if you are going to remove the affected area. The reason is that the disease might have spread to other parts. You won't know whether your tree is infected or not unless you see the disease start to show visible effects, but by then it might be too late to save the tree entirely.

If you are growing multiple bonsai trees, make sure that you do not place them together too closely. This restricts the movement of air and prevents adequate sunlight from reaching the plants. As discussed earlier, trees try to grab as much sunlight as possible. In some cases, the bonsais will start fighting for sunlight, becoming tangled up with each other and eventually harming each other.

Soil Conditions

You have to frequently check the soil conditions in the pot in order to ensure that your bonsai is growing well. Below, I have provided some of the ways in which you can check soil.

Basic Checks

One of the basic checks you have to perform is for water content. To do this, use a thin stick or material to carefully dig down to the root level. If you notice that the soil at that level is dry, then you are not provided adequate water. Many times – and this is particularly true for bonsai raised in deep pots – people might notice the dampness of the soil surface and think that they have provided sufficient water. Know that the roots of the bonsai require the water and if they are not getting it, then the tree won't be healthy.

Loose Soil

If the soil is loose either because of the repotting process, wind conditions in your area, or you were transporting the bonsai to another location, then don't immediately group the soil into the gaps.

If you do this, then there are chances of creating air pockets in the soil. What you should do instead is add fresh soil to the surface. Do note the soil type that is already present in the pot and match it. Using a stick or a similar device, start moving the newly added soil around the trunk slowly. Don't attempt to push as much soil into the hole as possible. Gently nudge the soil until the trunk is completely covered.

White Growth

Don't take actions out of panic. Always keep a level head as you analyze the situation. Here's an example. If you are planting hornbeams or pines, then the soil might start showing white mould-like growth on its surface. Many people immediately bring out fertilizers and pesticides in order to get rid of the mold and end up damaging the tree. In the species of trees I just mentioned, the white mold is actually a sign of good health. Do not touch it. However, that does not mean that all white loud presence is good for the bonsai. Know the difference. Take your time to evaluate the problem, if there is one. Speak to a professional or take the tree to the local garden store in order to receive informed advice.

Chapter 5

Styling and Shaping Your Bonsai

Now that the seedling is growing steadily, you are ready to grow your bonsai in a healthy and an attractive manner.

It's important to note that there is no such thing as a perfect bonsai, but you can get as close to perfection as possible. Since bonsai trees imitate nature, you should ensure that the proportions used for the tree you are growing reflect the proportions of the actual tree in the wild. You can achieve such results by constantly intervening during the growth of the tree and using various techniques like the ones mentioned below.

The whole process of raising your bonsai into the ideal shape is called "training."

Pruning

Let's begin with the tools of the trade. You need to have:

- Bud clippers
- Scissors. Ideally, I recommend having two types. One type has a short blade but long handles, while the other type has long and thick blades, but with short handles (the typical scissors you use for cutting paper). The long-handled scissors is used for removing buds, while the short-handled one is for cutting leaves.
- Branch cutters

If you are growing from seeds or using the propagation method, you need to start pruning the trees early. On the other hand, if you are using trees that you got from a store, then you can prune them later.

One of the best ways to prune, especially if you are growing a tree using a propagation method, is to cut branches on alternate sides. Start from the bottom and pick one side of the trunk. Call this Side A. The opposite side is Side B. You leave the first branch on Side A intact but cut off the first branch on Side B. Then leave the second branch on Side B intact while you cut off the second branch on Side A. Continue with the process for the remaining branches. Remember to this method only if it matches the style you are going for.

You are going to grow the tree into the shape you had in mind. Do not be hesitant about cutting branches that don't fit your shape. However, look at the branches and make a careful selection of those that you do not need. After all, once you cut a branch, it does not grow back. Some of the branches do not need careful consideration. One look at them and you know they are meant for the cutter. For example, if you would like to grow the tree in the Hokidachi style, then any branch closer to the root system needs to go.

When making cuts, remember to aim for a clean cut. I recommend having an isopropyl alcohol solution nearby to dip your pruning tools. When you dip your pruning tools into the alcohol solution, you disinfect them and prevent the spread of infections or diseases from one part of the plant to another. Other gardeners like to sterilize the pruning tool with fire. In the absence of alcohol, heat sterilization is an effective measure to kill any microbes that may have gotten on your tool. Ideally, you should sterilize the tool after each prune. I also prefer getting branch cutters with curved blades, since that ensures a clean cut.

When a branch is thick, you might find that it leaves behind a rather unattractive big hole behind once it is cut. To encourage faster healing, fill up the hole with grafting mastic.

You can also get Japanese tools for the pruning process. Fair warning: they aren't cheap. Their benefit is that they are especially made for bonsai trees.

Branch or Twig Pruning

Sometimes, branches need to be removed to achieve the style you desire. You will likely want to eliminate branches that cross each other or bend back toward the trunk as they make your bonsai look messy rather than artistic. Use concave branch cutters or bonsai shears, which will allow the tree to heal without damage or scars.

Debudding

When you first start to notice buds, you can pinch them with your fingernails. You usually perform this process at the beginning of springtime. After enough repetitions of the action, the tree will begin to produce smaller leaves. Make sure that you continue feeding the tree fertilizer based on its requirements.

Leaf Trimming

You don't have to perform this process on all trees. You only need to trim the leaves of those trees that have wide leaves, such as oaks and chestnuts. When it is late into spring, trim the leaves of the tree by half. Eventually, the tree starts growing smaller leaves. I would avoid trimming leaves if the tree is not healthy enough.

Shoot Pinching or Cutting

If you want to improve the quality of your tree's foliage, you need to maintain the shape of shoots. You can either choose to cut them or pinch them.

You can perform this type of pruning throughout the season if you note growth of new shoots or branches, especially those that make your plant look out of shape or unbalanced.

A word of caution here: be careful when you are pinching certain trees. They might have developed thorns and those could cause serious injuries. Usually, needles and thorns develop if you have not been pinching regularly. Examine the tree properly before pinching and if you notice needles or thorns, then switch to scissors.

During the maintenance of evergreens and conifers, you can make use of your fingers to pinch new growth. This is done in aim of encouraging fuller foliage and also to prevent browning.

Wiring

This is another important process for growing the right bonsai trees. The main reason for using wiring is to shift the shape of the tree away from its natural growth trajectory into a pattern that fits the shape you want to achieve.

Once again, we start with the necessary tools:

- Copper or brass wire
- Wire cutters to cut extra segments or make fine adjustments
- Pliers to get the shape that you want

TIP

You can also use steel wires, but be mindful that they can develop rust especially since you are going to water the trees frequently. In order to wire the branch well, you need to work your way from the 'bottom' of the branch (the part that is attached to the trunk) and move upward. The wire will go around the branch in a spiral pattern.

You should not keep the wire too loose or you might not get the shape you want. However, tie it too deep and you might cut into the branch. This can harm the branch, often strangling it. I recommend regularly removing the wire and then adding it back again as this can prevent the wire from digging into the branch or leaving permanent marks. For deciduous trees, you should keep the branches wired anywhere from eight to ten months. If you are working with coniferous trees, then the wire should be kept in place for anywhere from five to six months. When I say that the wire should be in place a certain duration, I don't mean that you can't remove it and add it back again. Rather, I am giving the duration for the entire wiring process. Ideally, you should attempt to bend the branch into the shape that you want it to take, then tie the wire around it.

Here are the steps to follow to wire your bonsai tree properly:

- The thickness of the wire will depend on the thickness of the part you wish to wire. Get a wire that is almost 1/3 of the thickness of the branch you wish to bend or style. You can get an aluminum wire from an old electrical cable but if you don't have access to any, you can always buy one from your local bonsai shop.
- To wire well, you need to anchor one end of the wire properly. You can do this by pushing the end of your wire into the soil.
- If you have never wired before, it would be wise to start wiring with a dead branch or even other garden shrubs before you can get working on your bonsai tree. Practicing with branches or shrubs allows you to gain more confidence in the process before you can move on to actual trees.
- When coiling the wire onto the branch, ensure you keep the turns at an angle of about 45 degrees. Also make sure that the wire is firm on the branch.

Some of the mistakes done when wiring a bonsai tree include:

- Coils of the wire being made too close or tight, which in turn will limit the flow of sap in the branch, effectively killing it.
- The wire being coiled too open, which in turn have insufficient power to hold the branch in place.
- The wire being coiled too loosely, in which there will be no effect on the branch.

After wiring, you will have to wait for a few months for the tree to get used to the new position before you can remove the wire. The amount of time needed to keep the wire on will depend on the type of tree being wired and the time of the year. Always keep a close eye on your tree; if you notice that the wire is starting to become too tight on the branch, cut it off. If one of the wired branches springs back, then you will have to rewire it. Don't leave the wire on the branch for so long that it starts cutting grooves into the bark.

Ageing

In order to age the bonsai, one of the options is to get an old tree, which can actually be rather costly.

Another method is to age the tree yourself. Many people harbor the misconception that ageing means forcing the tree to grow old fast. That is not true. The 'aged' appearance of the tree can be accomplished using some rather simple techniques.

To begin with, the tools:

- A scalpel
- Grafting knife
- Sandpaper

One of the techniques that you can use is known as 'jin.' In this process, you can either give a small part of or the entire trunk, or even a branch, the effect of wood that has been affected by time. In order to get that effect, you need to remove a strip of bark. Once done, take a piece of sandpaper and then rub the area you stripped. This will polish the trunk or branch well.

Once you have followed the above steps, you can make use of either a souring solution or citric acid and apply it on the stripped section and a little around it. Do not apply too much solution or acid, or else it might end up going deep into the tree, which can be fatal to it.

Most people might look at the result and think that the tree is not receiving the adequate supply of nourishment. But that is not true. The bark is simply an outer covering; it isn't a living component of the tree. You can use the above technique multiple times on the same tree, but I recommend limiting the number of sections that receive the ageing process. Try to plan out how you would like the result to look like and using the least amount of strips, try to achieve that result.

Trimming

Once you have attained the desired shape for your tree, you need to use the process of trimming to remove any unnecessary buds. You are not going to pinch these buds since you are not encouraging their growth; you are going to completely remove them.

The tools you might require for the trimming:

- Pincers
- Scissors

Trees such as cypress and needle juniper require constant trimming. For such trees, you have to firmly hold the branch, find the shoot that you want to remove, grab it using the pincers, and finally slowly twist. Take your time with the process. Make sure that you are not harming other shoots. For fruit and flowering trees, you have to work on them after you notice them flowering. When these trees begin to show new flowers on shoots that you don't want, you can trim those shoots to not only get rid of the unwanted section, but to encourage increased flowering.

Manuring

The process of manuring is often overlooked when growing bonsai trees. I cannot stress enough the importance of a good manuring routine. During spring and summer, I recommend that you allot one day just for manuring. Every week, on the same day, you should focus on applying manure to your soil. If you do not apply manure properly, then you might notice that the leaves might not have the lush green color that they should. Rather, many – if not most or all – of the leaves can turn pale. Additionally, if you are growing fruit or flowering trees, they will begin to have sparse blossoms.

Do not use the manure that is used on farms or gardens as they might be too heavy for bonsai. You can easily get lighter varieties. However, I should warn you about the smell of such light manures.

This won't be a problem if you keep the bonsai outdoors. But for indoor trees, you may want to find odorless versions of the manure.

When you get natural manures, then you are choosing from one of two types: animal manures or vegetable manures. Each type comes in paste, liquid, or powdered form. I do not recommend using the powdered form, unless the tree is still in the training phase. For bonsai that have grown to become small trees, powdered manure can affect the tree's appearance.

You can use paste. Just note that you should ideally allow it to mature for a week in hot weather, else the odor emanating from the manure can become quite strong. During cold weather, you can keep the manure for about a month. When using a paste, you should place it at the edge of the pot, as far away from the trunk as possible.

As for liquid manure, you can water the plants with the solution once a week starting from spring, all the way until autumn.

Choosing the Pot

If the bonsai is a picture, the pot is the frame. When the bonsai has grown into a tree, it's time to transfer it into a pot. You should pick the shape and the size of the pot based on those of the plant.

Here are a few tips to keep in mind when selecting the pot:
- If you picked a shape where the tree is leaning in one direction or cascading downwards such as the Fukinagashi or Kengai styles, then a circular pot will complement the styles wonderfully. Plant the tree in the center and allow the branches to cross the edges of the pots, if that is possible. Make sure you don't choose a wide circular pot for the cascading style, since you want the tree to have an 'overflow' effect, as though it is reaching out of the pot.
- A circular pot is also ideal for trees that have curves. For upright trees, a square pot complements the structure well.

- When it comes to the depth of the plot, the rule of thumb to keep in mind is that trees with dense foliage and thick trunks should have a deep pot, while trees with less foliage and thin trunks should have comparatively shallow pots.
- If you notice that the branches are growing longer on one side, don't hesitate to offset the tree in the pot. It does not necessarily have to be in the center. You can allow as much area of soil for the long branch to cover.
- When choosing the color of the pot, try to think of what could complement the tree. If your tree has thick foliage or if you are growing fruits or flowers, then you can use a green pot. You can also make use of colored pots, matching the color of the pot to the color of the fruit or flower. The main reason for doing this is to enhance the visuals of the tree. However, for deciduous and pine trees, do not use pots that have bright colors or too many designs. The focus should be on the tree and not the pot.

Image: Your choice of pot can have a big impact on the final presentation.

One of the tricks that I use for choosing the right pot is to step away from the tree. Since we work in close proximity to the tree, we need to step away to examine its overall visual appeal. When you examine it from afar, you have a better idea about what you can do to enhance the tree's visuals. Don't hesitate to consult with online sources. Browse through bonsai tree pictures to get an idea of what kind of pots others around the world are choosing for their trees.

When you have trained your bonsai well, you have only completed a part of the work. You still have to take care of the bonsai, and we are going to understand how in the next chapter.

Chapter 6

Pest, Infection, and Disease Remedies

Despite bonsai being such a unique representation of nature, it still falls prey to the effects of natural predators, just like any other plant, herb, or tree. And by natural predators, I am referring to pests and diseases. We are going to cover a range or pests and diseases in a bit, but I wanted to highlight an important activity that many people overlook. Too often, gardeners think about the cure. But I honestly believe that prevention is always better than the other, and unpleasant, option.

One of the best preventive measures is through the simple act of cleaning. After you prune the tree, repot it, or perform any other activity, then clean the top of the soil of any debris or plant materials. Most of the time, the materials that accumulate on the soil decompose. If they do, then they cause infections to spread to the trees. Some of these infections can cause the tree to die. Think about it, you can prevent your tree from dying by simply cleaning the space around it.

There are special brooms that you can get for the purpose. However, a simple brush can do the trick. Just make sure that the bristles of the brush are not too strong, or else they can dust off the top soil.

If you notice any weeds growing on the soil, then do not pull them out using your bare hands. Rather, use tweezers to pull them out. This is a slow process, but it preserves the health of your soil, and that is more important than picking a method that cuts corners.

People have added moss and grass into their pots to make the composition look livelier. I admit that moss and grass do make your bonsai look attractive, but I will warn you about the challenges.

Image: Adding moss, grass, and small growth may look pretty, but it is challenging.

The first is that if you are not careful – and by that, I mean really careful – then moss or grass can easily attract pests and diseases. I have had people look at pictures of bonsai and exclaim how lovely the addition of moss looked. They wanted to use moss themselves, but I mentioned to them an important fact about the pictures they saw; in most cases, the people who used moss have been raising bonsai for years. They have an intricate experience when it comes to dealing with bonsai. They know what they are doing. Beginners are not going to be able to manage so many different components of bonsai care.

The second challenge is in that moss and grass also require nutrients. They will take the nutrients available in the soil, which means that you have to be even more vigilant about the nutritional levels of the soil. If you make a single mistake, then you might have to repot the tree and get rid of all the moss and grass you had added.

Insecticides

Sometimes, despite how much you want to avoid them, you end up needing to use insecticides. The question is, what insecticides should you get in order to treat a pest problem?

One of the most common ingredients you should look out for is pyrethrum. This ingredient is sometimes mixed with rotenone or with agricultural nicotine. You can choose any combination you like, and the insecticide is fairly easy to obtain at your local garden supplies store.

You can also prepare insecticide at home. However, I do recommend wearing gloves, a mask, and even an apron, if you have one. It is better to protect yourself, since you are going to be dealing with chemicals after all. I am not saying that the insecticide is going to burn through your skin, but it might cause allergic reactions or rashes.

What you require is the below ingredients:

- Water - 1 liter
- Sulphur - 225 grams
- Quicklime - 112 grams

Simply mix all the ingredients together until you get a solution. You can also prepare a milder version of the solution by using the below measurements

- Water - 1 liter
- Sulphur - 25 grams
- Quicklime - 12.5 grams

The stronger solution can be used on trees after they have matured enough, while the weaker solution can be used on seedlings. Insecticide will be useful to deal with the biggest threat to a healthy bonsai: pests.

Pests

Here are some pests that you have to be aware of.

Ants

Most people are not aware of this fact about ants, but there are over 12,000 species of them spread across the globe. I bet we could come up with a handful of species and we usually name them as black or red ants. But imagine 12,000 different species of them.

Image: Ants harm the soil more than the tree itself.

By themselves, they do not do much harm. To the tree, that is. They are capable of plenty of harm to humans. I recommend that you always get rid of ants in your house in a timely manner, even if they are not approaching your tree.

But I just mentioned that they don't do any harm by themselves, so why should one remove them from trees? Well, it is because they carry bugs and aphids with them. And while they don't cause harm in the tree, they are capable of plenty of harm to the soil. If they make a home in the soil, then they can multiply fast.

If there is no nest, then you can spray an insecticide solution, preferably the nicotine and pyrethrum combination. However, if you do not have access to the insecticide, then try to make the solution I mentioned earlier using sulphur. You need to spray the insecticide on the tree, not pour it. If you are buying insecticide, then they usually come with a sprayer. In the absence of a sprayer, use your regular water sprayer. But once you use the sprayer at home, just put it away in a spot dedicated for gardening equipment. A fellow gardener once confessed to me that he almost used the pesticide sprayer for ironing his clothes. It was pure luck that his wife was already ironing the clothes and he noticed she was using another sprayer. Then, it dawned on him that the one in his hands was one filled with harmful chemicals. Be extra vigilant about what you are about to do.

If the ants have nested, you will need to repot the tree. Begin by following the procedures mentioned in the repotting section. Prune any roots that you think need to go, and then spray some of the insecticide slightly. I want you to be extra careful in this phase. You are holding the tree in your hands and the spray mist can spread in the air. To prevent a wide dispersion, bring the nozzle of the sprayer close to the roots and give a quick squeeze of the trigger. Alternatively, you can fill up a container with the insecticide solution, and then dip the roots in for about five to ten minutes. I would also recommend placing the container with the solution and the pot close together so that you don't drop pests onto the floor when transferring from pot to solution.

As for the old soil, discard it immediately, preferably as far away from home as possible. In order to prevent the pests from harming anybody or anything else, you can also burn the soil to get rid of the pests. After all, while the insects might scatter away, each one is capable of carrying a disease with it. You can burn the soil by sifting it into fire. You can even make use of a small tool to scrape off any soil still lodged in the pot. Disinfect the pot by spraying it generously with insecticide.

You usually spot ants during late spring all the way until early autumn. But do not be aware only during the aforementioned period. Keep your insecticide ready in case they attack your plant at other times of the year.

Aphids

Aphids are small bugs that live on trees. Unlike ants, they are dangerous for your bonsai because they suck the sap from the leaves. But that's not the only fact that makes them dangerous. Aphids are capable of reproducing quickly and they do so asexually. Yes indeed. They are big trouble. These pests produce young ones and those young ones in turn produce their own offspring within a short time. Before you know it, you have a colony of aphids on your tree happily turning your hard work into a buffet.

And there is more.

It is difficult to remove or get rid of aphids without insecticides. Veterans may be able to do so, but even they cannot be 100% successful sometimes. This is because aphids are small and come in brown, yellow, or green colors. The green ones are especially troublesome because they can sit on the leaves and at a casual glance, you might miss the fact that they are even there on the tree. Typically, they don't multiply in one single area. They form small clusters all over the plant or tree.

When they suck on the nutrients of the tree, they make the tree weaker. At such a weakened state, the tree becomes prone to diseases, infections, and even dehydration. Because they themselves become a source of food for other pests, they may even attract ants to build their colony in the tree. Yea, they are pretty nasty that way.

There are a few things that you can do to ensure that you get rid of them. The first is to spray the plant with insecticide. Do not worry about repotting the plant, since that won't be necessary. However, do spray lightly on the soil just to get rid of any aphids that might be roaming around the plant.

Once you have sprayed, make sure that you check – while wearing gloves – the various parts of the tree carefully for any signs of surviving aphids. Spray whenever you notice the pests.

You should also scrape off the old bark from the three. The best way to do this is by using a small knife and holding a little container just below the area you are scraping to collect any falling debris. Here is a step-by-step method to getting rid of aphids.

1. Spray the tree with the insecticide. Spray all the areas that you can think of.
2. Using gloved hands, start checking under branches and other hard-to-reach areas that the spray of insecticide might not have reached. If you notice any aphids still lingering about, give a quick spray.
3. Lightly spray on the top of the soil to get rid of any aphid not on the tree.
4. Start scraping off the bark to dislodge any aphid eggs. Collect the falling debris and eggs in an airtight container. Once you are done, seal the container tightly and get rid of it. You don't have to burn the container. Just seal all the pests inside.
5. Give a light mist on the tree right now in order to take care of any eggs you might have missed.

I have had people clean the container they used to collect the aphids so that they would use it again later. You can do this, should you prefer, but in order to clean it properly, you need to first use a proper soap solution. Once you have washed the container, dip it in insecticide solution and keep it there for about five to ten minutes. Once done, take it out and store it in a space that is specifically made for storing gardening supplies.

The above method should do the trick in most cases. But there is another way that is far more effective. If you can get your hands on methylated spirit, you can simply dip a cloth or a thick brush into the solution and then paint it all over the tree. This will get rid of any aphids, whether they are living or inside eggs.

Another point to remember is that if your tree starts to develop wool like formations – they mostly look like cotton wools – then you definitely have an aphid problem.

There is another sign to look for: ladybird beetles.

Image: Ladybirds not only help your plant, but they could add life to the bonsai.

However, if you do spot ladybird beetles, then you don't have to get rid of them. These beetles live off aphids. In fact, I have known people who introduce ladybirds to get rid of the aphid problem. I don't recommend this method for beginners because unless you know what you are doing, the process can take a long time and you might just end up watching your tree's health weaken.

Caterpillars

While these creatures eventually turn into beautiful butterflies, they have a voracious appetite. You might think a couple of caterpillars can't do much harm, but give them a couple of days and your beautiful green and brown tree will be mostly, if not entirely, brown. There are many species of caterpillars and once they attack the leaves of a tree, they destroy them until there are barely any signs of the leaves that were there before.

What makes these pests challenging to remove is that some of them have developed immunity toward insecticides. So simply spraying the tree is not going to get rid of them entirely. One of the best – and quite frankly, one of the most reliable – methods to use is to manually check the tree using gloved hands. If you spot a caterpillar, then you remove it. If you are using insecticide, then choose a powdered form that can stay on the leaves for a long period. This is done so that if any caterpillar does survive your scrutiny and starts eating the leaves, then it will consume the insecticide as well.

There is another trick you can use to catch them. Place a small bowl or saucer at the bottom of the tree and fill it with glue. Any caterpillar that gets stuck in the glue can be discarded. Do not apply the glue on the trees of the leaves. The glue might prevent that plant from breathing and suffocate it.

Boring Insects

Their name might probably give you an idea of what they are capable of, and yes, they can leave behind quite a bit of destruction in their wake. These pests can affect the health of your tree tremendously. The problem you might face with these insects is that once they have gotten under the bark of a tree, then they won't come out easily. You can make use of chemical insecticides, but often, they are too weak to have any effect. In other situations, they weaken the tree so much that even if you were to get rid of them, you might face an uphill battle trying to get your tree back to good health.

New gardeners have asked me why we don't get rid of them at the first sign of their presence? Why let them become such a nuisance in the end? Why can't we treat the boring insects problem before they start digging into the tree? The answer is quite simple; unless we have experience dealing with them, they are truly difficult to spot. For one, they don't leave behind big holes or gaps when they dig into the bark. The openings are small and most of the time, these openings look like they are part of the bark structure or design. It gets worse. For most of their lives, boring insects do not exit the hole. They don't need to get any fresh air or stretch their legs. They are quite comfortable remaining under the bark. It is only when you start to see the damage on the tree that you realize that you may have a serious problem. In other cases, many of the borer species don't live at the bottom or in the middle of the tree. They live in the uppermost sections of the tree, particularly where there are a lot of branches. This makes it even more difficult to spot them.

Despite the fact that boring insects are quite common in nature, their attack patterns are not commonly known. What I mean by this is that they don't usually attack healthy trees. They prefer to bore into weak or old trees. This means that the best preventive measures include taking care of the health of your tree, providing it adequate water and sunlight, and ensuring its nutritional levels are high.

Image: At a casual glance, you might not realize a boring insect is inside your bonsai.

When you keep your tree healthy, you give it a fighting chance. In that case, even if you happen to take some time to isolate the problem, your tree won't be affected as much as it could have been affected.

Sadly, there aren't many ways to check for boring insects other than trying to discover the holes they have created in the trees. They also leave behind slimy trains, which are their excretion; those are perhaps more obvious than the holes they create. But that shouldn't be a problem to you if you have been taking care of the tree regularly. You see, part of what makes regular care important is that not only does it prevent pests and diseases, but it allows you to get to know your tree better. Frequent care means you know the various changes that take place in the tree. That gap there? That was the one you made yourself in order to give an aged look to the tree. How about that hole? That's the remains of the branch you cut last week. And what about that hole? Now that one, you are not certain how it got there. It's best to get the insecticide out. Even small changes are easily discernible if you care for your tree regularly.

Now we come to the solution. In order to get rid of these pests, you need to take a syringe filled with insecticide and then pour the solution into the hole. Use the nicotine and pyrethrum combination for best effect. Once you have injected the solution into the tree, close the hole with clay. You can also make use of wax for the purpose of closing the hole. Remember that the number of injections is based on the size of the hole. If the hole is fairly large, then you might have to inject the insecticide multiple times in order to make it effective.

How can you tell if you have taken care of the boring insects? You need to pay attention to the tree. Over the course of the next few days or weeks, you should notice some or all of the below signs:

- The tree's health does not deteriorate any further
- There are no slimy trails left on the tree.

Boring insects mainly attack the tree from spring and all the way to autumn. You should focus your attention on the trunks and branches. Leave the soil as you will not find them there. However, you should also spray a light mist of insecticide on the soil as well.

Earthworms

Earthworms are not pests. Well, I think I should rephrase that. They are pests. But they are good pests.

They are more like pets, if you think about it. Except, you don't cuddle them or take them out for walks.

And they are pets of the bonsai, to be precise. Earthworms are good for the bonsai. They create passageways for the roots, which allows the roots to grow freely. They also mix up the nutrition and water content in the soil, spreading it all around so that the roots are able to absorb them better.

To get rid of them, you can use any of the pyrethrum solutions or the homemade insecticide mixture. For the most part, you should allow two or three earthworms to live in the pot, depending on the size of the pot. Don't allow the earthworms to crowd into the pot, since they actually end up eating a lot of the soil.

Oh, and you should also be aware of worm castings. These are one of the richest fertilizers that you can ever come across? What is worm casting?

Well, in short, it's worm poop. When earthworms eat through the soil, they also leave behind, well, their waste matter. This waste matter becomes natural fertilizer for the plants. How nutritious can worm castings be for the plant? Surely they can't be as good as real fertilizer, now can they? Let me put it this way. If you can get enough worm castings to barely fit a tablespoon, that matter can be used to provide nutrition to a 6-inch plant for two months. Yes indeed. They are that effective for plants.

Here is another benefit – yes, there are a few more. Worm castings can be more easily absorbed by the plant compared to artificial or animal manure, or fertilizer. The castings are also capable of reducing the chances of root rot from developing. Root rot is a disease where the roots of the plants begin to decay and rot. Additionally, worm castings are also able to retain water in the soil well, which is mainly possible because of their texture. Amazing!

There is one more benefit to earthworms besides their poop (can't believe I just said that). These worms are also capable of consuming any impurities or small creatures that have burrowed into the soil.

However, as with all things in life, too much of anything is not good. As I had recommended earlier, try to keep a maximum of three earthworms, since the more they are, the more castings are formed. This formation can present a rather ugly sight and can eventually turn the soil lumpy. But when in a controlled population, plants and trees love earthworms.

Larvae of May Beetles

These pests are active during late spring all the way into summer. They like to live deep in the soil and are therefore quite difficult to discover. Their bodies are shaped like a half-moon and they usually come in a yellowish-white color. These pests are dangerous to the roots of the tree since the creatures feed on roots.

I know what you might be thinking; time to get those earthworms. Not so fast. While adding earthworms is a good solution, there is no guarantee that the worms will be able to feed on the insects in time to prevent any damage. It is effective if you have already introduced earthworms into the soil prior to the presence of may beetles. By that time, the earthworms are long enough to have a good appetite and they can cover a wide distance easily.

If you haven't already introduced earthworms, then you need to repot the plant. Gently pull the plant or tree from the pot and then wash the soil. Once you have washed it, you can spray insecticide to clear away any beetles. At this point, I must mention that some may beetles can be resistant to insecticide, but it helps if you spray some on the roots since you can affect young beetles.

Once you have repotted the plant, dispose of the old soil in the same way mentioned in the section on ants. It is far better to burn the soil so that the pests don't spread into your garden, lawn, or other areas.

Mealy Bugs

Mealy bugs are usually found in warm climate regions. They resemble cotton buds and are very soft-bodied. They feed by sucking the nutrition or sap out from leaves. In small quantities, they don't cause a lot of damage. This is why you might not notice their presence (especially if they stick to the underside of a leaf) until they have grown to large numbers and have started attacking other parts of the bonsai. When the leaves begin to lose their health, they might either curl up or turn yellow. What makes these bugs a nuisance is the fact that they can lay anywhere from 300 to 600 eggs within a two week period, and most of those eggs are capable of hatching within the next week or two.

There are several ways to get rid of these bugs.

- You can introduce ladybirds, who are more than happy to 'feast' on the problem for you. You can even get commercially bought ladybirds in the market, should you need them.
- The other method is to simply use a Q-tip. Dip the Q-tip into an isopropyl alcohol solution and apply it on the bugs.
- If a certain part of the tree has already been infested, then prune out that part. Be careful when pruning, so that you don't allow the infested part to fall into the pot. A simple pruning method would be to place a container below the target area and snip it off. Allow the pruned part to fall into the container, taking the bugs along with it.
- You can prevent the growth of these bugs by not overfertilizing your plants. Mealy bugs are attracted to high nitrogen content.
- Finally, spray the affected area with insecticides in order to get rid of the problem.

Red Spiders

Red spiders can be a big problem if left unchecked. They can affect your bonsai and they are also not good to have around the house.

The term 'spider' is a bit of a misnomer here. In fact, spiders can actually be beneficial to your plant – more on that later. Red spiders are actually a type of mite. The word spider is used because of the shape of the mite, which almost resembles that of an arachnid. That and the fact that these mites have eight legs and can produce webs. Because of these features, they are placed in the spider category.

Red spiders are mainly active during the hot period of the year, especially when it gets a bit dry. However, that does not mean they don't affect plants during other seasons. During cold weather, they are found indoors, using the warmth of the house. Any indoor bonsai are affected during this period. When it is summer, they move outside and attack the bonsai. A simple method to prevent them from harming your bonsai is by keeping it outside during winter. However, that is a stop-gap solution and does not permanently get rid of the pests. These pests feast on the leaves and flowers of bonsai and in many cases, they destroy the parts of the bonsai entirely.

The first thing that you have to do is isolate the bonsai. Keep it away from the indoors. You can then use the sulphur solution or the nicotine and pyrethrum solution to get rid of them. As always, spray the insecticide on them. You won't be able to get rid of them after the first spray of insecticides. You will need to repeat the treatment every three days for at least twelve to fifteen days.

If you can prevent their spread on time, you may be able to avoid serious damage to your bonsai. However, if the pests have already damaged the leaves and fruits, then bear in mind that it might take up to three years for the bonsai to recover from the attack. This fact is important because gardeners do not see improvements in their bonsai within a short period after the pests have been taken care of. This causes the gardeners to falsely diagnose the bonsai as being unhealthy. They then proceed to get rid of the bonsai. But do not make such a diagnosis unless you have consulted a professional gardener.

Scale Insects

These pests are oddly shaped and resemble a bump. They are mostly immobile, choosing to stick to a particular part of the plant and slowly suck out the nutrition from it. They can go unnoticed until there is a buildup of a huge colony of scale insects all over the tree.

When these pests reach adult stage, then they start laying eggs underneath their shell. After some time, typically before three weeks, the eggs hatch and young scale insects begin to crawl out. These young ones are highly mobile because they are looking for the ideal site to attach to and start their feeding process, after which the cycle of laying eggs and creating new scale insects continues.

Here are a few ways to get rid of the insects:

- If you notice a large part of a branch or leave infected by these pests, then prune out that part. Make sure that you place a container below the area you prune.
- If the number of insects is still low, you can just remove them using gloved hands and then mist the bonsai with your insecticide. You may need to spray several times before you get rid of them. Follow the instructions provided under the mealy bugs section for the best way to use the insecticide.

Diseases

Let's examine the common diseases that can affect your bonsai. We start off with the one that most people might recognize – mildew.

Powdery Mildew

Mildew is caused by fungus. It is easily recognizable because it develops into a white coating. No bonsai is immune to mildew disease but there are some plants, especially the flowering ones, that attract milden more than others.

You would be surprised to know that mildew comes in several varieties, but since they all have similar powdery appearance, it can be hard to distinguish between the various types. It should be noted that if you are growing several bonsai and mildew has affected one plant, then it is unlikely that it will spread to other plants, unless all the bonsai you are growing are of the same type: this is because mildew attacks specific plants. For example, if there is a mildew attacking your citrus bonsai, then it won't attack another bonsai belonging to a different family. However, that does not mean that the unaffected plants are free from danger. They can develop their own mildew infestation.

While mildew is quite unattractive to look at, it doesn't pose terrible danger to the plants in the short-run. What I mean by that is that it's not like with pests, where they start consuming the part of the tree they infect. In the long run, mildew could cause harm since it can cause stress to the plant. If the bonsai becomes infected more than once, then it tends to become weaker. A weak bonsai is like a lantern attracting all manner of other diseases and pests.

To remove mildew from your tree, you can do any of the following:

- Use plant clippers to remove the infected area entirely. This might not be an ideal solution, but if the area has been affected severely by the infection, this is an option you can consider. Make sure that you keep a container filled with a water and soap solution, or a container with isopropyl alcohol. Once you have used the clippers on the trees, make sure you dip them into the solution so that you clean them.
- Another method to get rid of the disease is to use a fungicide. When choosing the fungicide, you should look for ingredients such as copper, neem oil, or potassium bicarbonate. These are all ingredients that can help you rid of your mildew problem efficiently.

However, your work does not end with the removal of mildew. Now that you know that a certain bonsai was affected, you need to take preventive measures to ensure mildew does not return to the same plant. Here are some steps you can take:

- Prune the tree properly so that there is enough circulation for all areas of the bonsai.
- Make sure that you have treated the problem completely before you do anything else to the plant. For example, avoid using fertilizers until the bonsai has been rid of the mildew and you have used fungicide. Mildew prefers plants that have a high level of nutrition, which occurs when they take in fertilizers.
- Provide the right conditions for bonsai growth. If you are keeping the bonsai indoors, then make sure that they do not suffer the effects of humidity. Keep windows open and allow fresh air to circulate throughout the house.

Rust

This disease is also caused by fungus, but takes on a brownish or orangish color. Remember that prevention is always better, so make sure that you are taking care of the bonsai to avoid rust from ever appearing. But if it happens despite your best efforts, then you can use the following steps:

- Remove the parts of the bonsai that are infected.
- Remove any debris on the soil or between branches.
- Use a fungicide to get rid of the spread of fungus.

Once you have cleaned away the presence of rust from the bonsai, do not water the plants. Water can transport the fungus from one part to another.

After you have dealt with the rust problem, follow the preventive techniques mentioned in the mildew section.

Image: Discoloring of the leaves is one way of recognizing rust.

Diseases Caused by Nutrient Deficiency

There are many diseases that spread because of lack of nutrition to the bonsai. Diseases such as chlorosis or magnesium deficiency occur because the bonsai is not fed the right food. When deficiency affects bonsai, the solution is not a matter of spraying the tree with insecticide or fungicide, or cutting of the affected areas.

- If you have already been giving fertilizer to the bonsai, then you need to check the type of fertilizer used. Change fertilizers in order to prevent further damage.
- However, if the problem is the lack of fertilizer, then make sure that you start creating a feeding schedule. The schedule will help you feed your plants at regular intervals and prevent further instances of deficiency.

- Check sunlight and water supply. Usually, lack of water causes dehydration; that dehydration can in turn attract diseases as well.
- Check the humidity levels in the area and see if they are affecting your bonsai. Sometimes the leaves might start turning dry. Immediately provide the right amount of water in order to nourish the plants. However, do note that humidity provides the perfect condition for the growth of other diseases, such as mildew and rust. You should look to increase the ventilation in the space.

Root Rot

We have mentioned root rot earlier. It is a slow decay of the roots and it kills the bonsai tree entirely. But what causes it?

One of the main reasons for its presence is the quality of the fertilizer. If you do not purchase your fertilizer from good sources, then you are likely to get something that has already decomposed a fair bit. Adding decomposed fertilizer to the soil is only going to cause more problems to it.

Root rot is a fungus. And by now, that fact might not surprise you one bit. If you have been watering your plants well, then the roots won't suffer the problem. However, if you have been adding too much water to the roots, then they might develop root rot. Remember that overwatering does not happen only because you added extra water. It is also possible because there is a lack of proper drainage system. This prevents water from leaking out of the pot.

The biggest problem with root rot is identifying it. Since it affects the roots, you may not know how much damage the bonsai has suffered unless you take out the plant and carefully examine it, which is why I strongly recommend that you create the ideal growing conditions for the plant from the very beginning. Check the fertilizer quality and expiry date. Get to know exactly how much water you need to add to the plant and maintain a proper watering schedule.

But what can you do if the root rot has already affected your plants? In that case, there is no easy solution. The best option available to you is to remove the infected areas. However, that could pose another problem; your bonsai is going to have insufficient roots to take in the nutrition from the soil.

You should also clean out the infected soil from the roots. Add in fresh soil and compost to the container or choose to repot the plant. I personally prefer the latter option since it gives me more peace of mind.

Chapter 7

Style Guide

If you prefer, you can choose a full-grown bonsai that has been raised under the best conditions possible. But apart from the obvious factor of the pricing of the bonsai, just what tree should you choose for your space?

While I am dedicating this chapter to picking a fully-grown bonsai, you can also use this information to help you decide what kind of bonsai you would like to grow in your house.

Choosing the Right Style of Bonsai

Each bonsai comes with its own set of requirements. Some need more attention than others.

Image: Some bonsai require more attention than others.

Think about how much time you can allot to taking care of your bonsai. If you feel that you can set aside a couple of hours or more every day to carefully look after your bonsai, then you can avoid the beginner bonsai trees. However, I recommend getting a strong foothold in the bonsai world by choosing a beginner bonsai as your first tree. Some of the options available to you are the juniper bonsai and of course, the ficus bonsai. The ficus is especially beginner-friendly and highly popular in the bonsai community. Even people who have been growing bonsai for a long time enjoy growing the ficus, since people experience less stress growing the tree.

Then there are the leaves. Are you comfortable trimming the leaves in order to maintain a small size? If you are not, then you should go for the Chinese elm tree, which already has small leaves. You will still have to trim the leaves; however, the process isn't as intense or extensive as the ones you use for other bonsai.

Do you want to add a bit of color but prefer to work on a simple tree? Then try working on the maple bonsai. Do note that maple bonsais do pose a fair bit of challenge, but if you can carefully raise them, then you won't have any problem growing a wonderful maple.

Also, you should think about the size. If you are comfortable having a plant sized bonsai, then try going for the Dwarf Schefflera. This bonsai is not only easier to raise, but is a beautiful decorative piece. You can easily place it on your window sill or on a small table.

The Jade bonsai is another option: it is fairly larger than the Dwarf Schefflera, but still almost plant-sized. This bonsai is easy to grow, but it requires a fairly high amount of sunlight.

Lastly, consider whether you want an indoor or outdoor bonsai. Juniper bonsai is an indoor tree, but the Jade bonsai, since it requires plenty of sunlight, is an outdoor tree.

Think about these factors before you pick the ideal bonsai for you. We already mentioned a few bonsai options. Let's now look at them in detail.

Juniper

This is the most used bonsai tree by beginners since it can be shaped easily to look like old pine trees. The most recommended type of juniper tree is the *Juniper procumbens* 'Nana.' You should note that this tree is not an indoor plant.

Ficus

This bonsai tree is among the best for beginners especially if you want to grow an indoor bonsai. Most of the varieties of ficus bonsai trees are good for bonsai growing.

Chinese Elm

It is also known as *Ulmus Parvifolia*. This tree type can be easily restyled and trimmed. It has perfect, small leaves and a root system that resembles strings. This makes it good for growing as a rock plant. It can be grown indoors since it adapts quickly.

Dwarf Schefflera

This tree is also known as arboricola/umbrella tree. This tree is a good indoor bonsai tree for beginners.

The Jade Bonsai Tree

This tree type is also a good bonsai indoor tree that has small leaves.

What to Look for when Choosing a Bonsai Tree

Whether you opt to start your bonsai tree with an already existing tree or use a seedling, it is best to have some important points in mind when buying or looking for your tree.

Healthy Plant

This is the first consideration you should make when choosing a bonsai tree. At times, you might get tempted by how nicely shaped a tree looks and forget about its health. A healthy tree should have green leaves (which is dependent on the time of the year), no signs of pests and should be stable in the container or pot.

Dead Branches or Scars

These signs are often associated with age and they are essential to make your bonsai tree look old, but it is not necessary to check for these when buying the tree since you can easily create them yourself. When creating the effect of age on your tree, make sure to give it a natural touch.

When in the garden or store, it is generally better not to accept trees that already look old even if the seller claims that they are decorative.

First Branch

For upright bonsai plants, you need to consider the condition of the first branch. A good first branch should be about one third of the final size of the tree. You should also ensure that it is the heaviest of all the branches on your bonsai.

Lots of Branches

When you want to acquire a starter bonsai plant, look for one that has a lot of branches. However, you will not need all of them, it will help you find the best ones after eliminating the bad ones.

Nebari

This term is Japanese and it refers to the surface roots of trees that shoot out from the trunk. This feature is valued highly for bonsai trees as it adds an aged look to the trees.

Proportion

The flower, fruits and leaves must be proportional to the final height. For instance, if you want to create a small bonsai tree, choosing a tree with small leaves would be best to bring out the small tree-look. You should also consider the size of the flowers and fruits the tree bears since they can also affect the miniature look of your bonsai tree.

Taper

This is where the trunk of your tree is narrow at the top and widens downwards towards the roots. The branches of the tree should also be narrower towards the tip. Trees with branches that have a shape resembling poles are bad for growing as bonsai.

Tree Type

Choose a tree type that will work well depending on your requirements. You should also keep in mind that not all types of popular trees are good to grow as bonsai trees.

Trunk

If you are going to start growing your bonsai from an already existing tree, you also need to check its trunk to ensure that it is 'heavy'. This gives the tree an older look.

As you get started, it is critical to understand that bonsai isn't just a "one size fits all" kind of thing. You can implement it differently by following different bonsai styles that we'll talk about shortly.

How Should You Display It?

It is important to note that most bonsai are outdoor plants. Just like the trees in the forest, you shouldn't keep bonsai inside the house for too long. Even indoor bonsai should have sufficient sunlight.

However, it is understandable that you would like to display the bonsai indoors. For that, here are a few guidelines you should follow based on the Japanese way of displaying bonsai.

- Bonsai is usually placed in the main room of the house, most likely the living room.
- It should be placed against a wall that is devoid of any other form of decorations other than the ones I will recommend further in this section. Lighting is allowed, but it should be used only to illuminate the bonsai.
- The bonsai can be accompanied by a scroll that features Japanese writing. The scroll should be placed on the wall behind the bonsai. Make sure that the scroll is large. How large you would like it to be depends on your personal preference.

Image: There are many ways to display your bonsai.

- Bonsai should be placed in the special container that you have picked for the tree. Additionally, they should never be placed directly on the ground. You can choose a small base of a table to hold the bonsai.
- Here is a simple presentation format as an example: The scroll is in the center of the exhibit, the bonsai sits to its right on a table, and a smaller plant or another bonsai is placed to its left.

- If you have a single bonsai, allow it to occupy a space in front of the center of the wall. On either side of it, you can place scrolls or works of art. The art should not contain too many colors because they can distract the viewer from examining the bonsai.
- If you have a small bonsai, place it on a pedestal-like platform. Alternatively, choose a fireplace or a table in the main room such as a coffee table surrounded by many sofas. Allow the bonsai to be the centerpiece of your preferred choice of platform. Do not adorn the platform with other objects, unless they are bonsai trees as well.

Presentation Tip

Remember that the above guidelines are there to help you get a general impression on how to display your bonsai. However, it does not mean that they have to be followed precisely.

For example, you can place a bonsai on the coffee table on one end and a small decorative piece like a statue on the other, preferably one that is silver-colored. The contrast of colors between the two objects can be quite mesmerizing. However, that is just one suggestion. You can choose to ignore all the guidelines above in order to create your ideal display. Do not be afraid to experiment.

The Formal Style

This style follows traditions established by the Japanese. While the style varies from one person to another, there are certain principles that are shared between each bonsai presentation.

While you can choose practically any bonsai to help you achieve the formal style, the best trees to make use of are spruces and pines, as the trunks of the trees are nearly straight and tapered.

In the formal style, the presentation of the tree is the sole focus, so the pot should not steal the attention from the tree. When choosing a pot, look for ones with an earthy color such as the natural brown of soil or those that have a greyish-brown tint. The shape of the pot should ideally be rectangular or square.

If you are displaying the bonsai in a room, the formal style demands that you do not adorn the room with decor such as ornamental lighting fixtures, wallpapers with complex designs, too many electronic devices, or a large number of furniture.

The principles provide ample room to modify the display style of the bonsai. Some people choose to keep simple-patterned wallpapers while others avoid wallpapers, choosing instead to use a carpet that matches the aesthetics of the bonsai. As long as you maintain the principles of the formal style in your decor, you can get fairly creative with the display of your bonsai.

The Semi-Formal Style

Anytime you artificially change the shape of the branches of the bonsai tree, you have created a semi-formal style. It does not matter if you haven't changed the shape too much, maybe only adjusting the direction of one branch. But as long as you alter the natural growth of the tree, then you have formed a semi-formal style.

What does this mean in terms of presentation?

The choice of containers, for one, is going to be fairly unique to the style. You can choose oval, petal, or even hexagonal containers. Make sure that whatever you choose, it fits the tree you are growing.

There isn't really a perfect container for a specific tree, so my recommendation is to think about how your tree will look in a particular container, and then imagine that container in the space that you would like it in. Ask yourself the questions below:

- Can you imagine the tree and container in that location?
- Does it provide the best view for a visitor?
- Are there many objects distracting it?
- Does it take a lot of space?

As for the color of the pot, an earthy color is ideal. However, for certain deciduous trees or for bonsai such as maple, you can choose a container to match the leaves. The effect can be quite striking.

I would recommend the following:

- Plan early. Think about the space where you would like to place your bonsai. What is the color of the wall? You can then choose a tree accordingly.
- Alternatively, you can change the wall color based on the bonsai you are growing.

Whether you choose a bonsai to complement the wall or change the wall color to complement the bonsai, do not match the colors of the wall and bonsai. If you do so, then it creates an effect where your bonsai's leaves blend into the color of the wall. While that may sound pleasing in theory, it creates a distracting effect in reality.

The choice of color does not merely refer to the wall, but to the surrounding objects. You can either take the safe route by picking up brown or dark brown sculptures or items, or choose an object with complementing color.

I also recommend looking at the presentation of your home. Is your home splashed with a lot of colors, whether from the decor or paint? Then it would really look odd if just one of your rooms was plain in order to accommodate a bonsai. I say, add more color! Create a vibrant look for your home. Don't hold back after you have already added a lot of color to your home.

A bonsai is a long-term investment. Plan out in advance before you think about getting a tree.

Informal Style

When you pick *The Literati Style*, *The Forest Style*, or *The Growing on a Rock Style*, then you are picking bonsai trees that fall into the informal style of presentation. When you choose an informal style, your main idea might probably be to add a unique presentation to your home: you want to break rules, or perhaps add an abstract style of decor in your room.

The first point to note about the informal style is that you should ideally pick containers that have intricate designs or even simple art. You might also come across certain pots that have a bright glaze on them: they make wonderful additions for your bonsai tree.

The informal style is commonly found in Western homes since these homes do not have Japanese alcoves or any of the popular Japanese decor. In the absence of such decor, the informal style is used to create bonsai ideal for a certain type of home or interior.

I recommend that since there are such unique bonsai in the informal style, you should try to place them on a table. Such a placement allows their beauty to be isolated, as though you are presenting a prized possession.

Harvesting for Your Kitchen

Finally, a quick note on harvesting bonsai for your kitchen: Do not place any flowering bonsai in the kitchen. I cannot stress on this enough. If pests and diseases affect the bonsai, then they can spread to other parts of the kitchen and that is not something you want to deal with.

Keep flowering bonsais outside. In fact, nearly every flowering bonsai requires adequate sunlight anyways. When the fruits are ready for picking, pluck them gently. Immediately discard any fruit that has been affected by pests or looks like it might have contracted a disease. How do you know if it has a disease? It will have strange spots all over it or it might not be as colorful as the other fruits.

Always wash the fruits and other food picked from the bonsai properly.

But most importantly, enjoy the fruits of your labor (no pun intended).

Conclusion

Bonsai is a rewarding activity, if you have the patience for it. Bonsai is not just about growing a tree. The activity can be a great stress reliever. There is something truly relaxing and calming about the entire experience. It is why many people around the world are drawn to it as a hobby. I know people who use it instead of meditation and they swear by its effects. While I cannot claim to be an expert on meditation, I do know that that growing bonsai has a certain meditative quality to it.

Additionally, bonsai actually makes you a more patient person. It demands that you show it respect and wait for things to develop. If you are patient, you are going to see results. There is a great philosophy in bonsai care, one that talks about putting hard work in your endeavors and waiting for them to develop into something beautiful. This is true in nearly all aspects of life. Hard work is an important factor, but so is patience. Things shouldn't be rushed, or they might grow into something you might not like.

Image: People enjoy bonsai care for its meditative qualities.

Also, let's not forget that bonsai are one of the best adornments that you can get for your house, at least in my opinion. Not only are they beautiful, but they purify the air, creating a healthy and beautiful environment for your home.

I hope that you have a wonderful bonsai growing journey, and I equally hope that you grow a beautiful bonsai that lights up your house and also your life.

Before you close this book, I would love to know what you think about it.

If you liked the book, please leave a nice review for me. When I read your reviews, it makes me happy to know I have done a good job! I would be immensely thankful if you could go online now and write a quick line sharing with me your experience. I personally read all the reviews and I would be thrilled to hear your feedback and honest motivation. After all, it is what keeps me going and helps me to improve every day.

PS: Can I Ask You for a Quick Favor?

First of all, thank you for purchasing **Bonsai Book for Beginners**! I know that you could have picked any number of books to read, but you picked this one and for that I am extremely grateful.

If you enjoyed this book and found some benefit in reading it, I'd like to hear from you and hope that you could take some time to post a review if possible.

Your feedback and support will help me to greatly improve my writing craft for future projects and make this book even better.

THANKS!

:)

www.ingramcontent.com/pod-product-compliance
Lightning Source LLC
Chambersburg PA
CBHW071009080526
44587CB00015B/2402